ESOTERIC TEXTS

BDK English Tripiṭaka Series

ESOTERIC TEXTS

The Sutra of the Vow of Fulfilling the Great Perpetual Enjoyment and Benefiting All Sentient Beings Without Exception

(Taishō Volume 8, Number 243)

Translated by Taisen Miyata

The Mātaṅga Sutra

(Taishō Volume 21, Number 1300)

Translated by Rolf W. Giebel

The Bodhicitta Śāstra

(Taishō Volume 32, Number 1665)

Translated by Minoru Kiyota

Bukkyō Dendō Kyōkai America, Inc.
2015

Second Printing, 2018
ISBN: 978-1-886439-58-0
Library of Congress Control Number: 2015947185

Published by
BDK America, Inc.
1675 School Street
Moraga, California 94556

Printed in the United States of America

A Message on the Publication of the English Tripiṭaka

The Buddhist canon is said to contain eighty-four thousand different teachings. I believe that this is because the Buddha's basic approach was to prescribe a different treatment for every spiritual ailment, much as a doctor prescribes a different medicine for every medical ailment. Thus his teachings were always appropriate for the particular suffering individual and for the time at which the teaching was given, and over the ages not one of his prescriptions has failed to relieve the suffering to which it was addressed.

Ever since the Buddha's Great Demise over twenty-five hundred years ago, his message of wisdom and compassion has spread throughout the world. Yet no one has ever attempted to translate the entire Buddhist canon into English throughout the history of Japan. It is my greatest wish to see this done and to make the translations available to the many English-speaking people who have never had the opportunity to learn about the Buddha's teachings.

Of course, it would be impossible to translate all of the Buddha's eighty-four thousand teachings in a few years. I have, therefore, had one hundred thirty-nine of the scriptural texts in the prodigious Taishō edition of the Chinese Buddhist canon selected for inclusion in the First Series of this translation project.

It is in the nature of this undertaking that the results are bound to be criticized. Nonetheless, I am convinced that unless someone takes it upon himself or herself to initiate this project, it will never be done. At the same time, I hope that an improved, revised edition will appear in the future.

It is most gratifying that, thanks to the efforts of more than a hundred Buddhist scholars from the East and the West, this monumental project has finally gotten off the ground. May the rays of the Wisdom of the Compassionate One reach each and every person in the world.

NUMATA Yehan
Founder of the English
Tripiṭaka Project

August 7, 1991

Editorial Foreword

In the long history of Buddhist transmission throughout East Asia, translations of Buddhist texts were often carried out as national projects supported and funded by emperors and political leaders. The BDK English Tripiṭaka project, on the other hand, began as a result of the dream and commitment of one man. In January 1982 Dr. NUMATA Yehan, founder of Bukkyō Dendō Kyōkai (Society for the Promotion of Buddhism), initiated the monumental task of translating the complete Taishō shinshū daizōkyō edition of the Chinese Tripiṭaka (Buddhist canon) into the English language. Under his leadership, a special preparatory committee was organized in April 1982. By July of the same year the Translation Committee of the English Tripiṭaka was officially convened.

The initial Committee included the following members: (late) HANAYAMA Shōyū (Chairperson), (late) BANDŌ Shōjun, ISHIGAMI Zennō, (late) KAMATA Shigeo, (late) KANAOKA Shūyū, MAYEDA Sengaku, NARA Yasuaki, (late) SAYEKI Shinkō, (late) SHIOIRI Ryōtatsu, TAMARU Noriyoshi, (late) TAMURA Kwansei, (late) URYŪZU Ryūshin, and YUYAMA Akira. Assistant members of the Committee were as follows: KANAZAWA Atsushi, WATANABE Shōgo, Rolf Giebel of New Zealand, and Rudy Smet of Belgium.

After holding planning meetings on a monthly basis, the Committee selected one hundred and thirty-nine texts for the First Series of the project, estimated to be one hundred printed volumes in all. The texts selected were not limited to those originally written in India but also included works composed in China and Japan. While the publication of the First Series proceeds, the texts for the Second Series will be selected from among the remaining works; this process will continue until all the texts, in Japanese as well as in Chinese, have been published. Given the huge scope of this project, accomplishing the English translations of all the Chinese and Japanese texts in the Taishō canon may take as long as one hundred years or more. Nevertheless, as Dr. NUMATA wished, it is the sincere hope of the Committee that this project will continue until completion, even after all the present members have passed away.

Dr. NUMATA passed away on May 5, 1994, at the age of ninety-seven. He entrusted his son, Mr. NUMATA Toshihide with the continuation and completion of the English Tripiṭaka project. Mr. Numata served for twenty-three years, leading the project forward with enormous progress before his sudden passing on February 16, 2017, at the age of eighty-four. The Committee previously lost its able and devoted first Chairperson, Professor HANAYAMA Shōyū, on June 16, 1995, at the age of sixty-three. In October 1995 the Committee elected Professor MAYEDA Sengaku (then Vice President of Musashino Women's College) as Chairperson, and upon the retirement of Professor Mayeda in July 2016, the torch was passed to me to serve as the third Chairperson. Despite these losses and changes we, the Editorial Committee members, have renewed our determination to carry out the noble ideals set by Dr. NUMATA. Present members of the Committee are Kenneth K. Tanaka (Chairperson), MAYEDA Sengaku, ICHISHIMA Shōshin, ISHIGAMI Zennō, KATSURA Shōryū, NARA Yasuaki, SAITŌ Akira, SHIMODA Masahiro, WATANABE Shōgo, and YONEZAWA Yoshiyasu.

The Numata Center for Buddhist Translation and Research was established in November 1984, in Berkeley, California, U.S.A., to assist in the publication of the translated texts. The Publication Committee was organized at the Numata Center in December 1991. In 2010, the Numata Center's operations were merged with Bukkyō Dendō Kyōkai America, Inc. (BDK America), and BDK America continues to oversee the publication side of the English Tripiṭaka project in close cooperation with the Editorial Committee in Tokyo.

At the time of this writing, in February 2017, the project has completed about sixty percent of the seven thousand one hundred and eighty-five Taishō pages of texts selected for the First Series. Much work still lies ahead of us but we are committed to the completion of the remaining texts in order to realize the grand vision of Dr. Numata, shared by Mr. Numata and Professor Hanayama, to make the Buddhist canon more readily accessible to the English-speaking world.

Kenneth K. Tanaka
Chairperson
Editorial Committee of
the BDK English Tripiṭaka

Publisher's Foreword

On behalf of the members of the Publication Committee, I am happy to present this volume as the latest contribution to the BDK English Tripiṭaka Series. The Publication Committee members have worked to ensure that this volume, as all other volumes in the series, has gone through a rigorous process of editorial efforts.

The initial translation and editing of the Buddhist scriptures found in this and other BDK English Tripiṭaka volumes are performed under the direction of the Editorial Committee in Tokyo, Japan. Both the Editorial Committee in Tokyo and the Publication Committee, headquartered in Moraga, California, are dedicated to the production of accurate and readable English translations of the Buddhist canon. In doing so, the members of both committees and associated staff work to honor the deep faith, spirit, and concern of the late Reverend Dr. Yehan Numata, who founded the BDK English Tripiṭaka Series in order to disseminate the Buddhist teachings throughout the world.

The long-term goal of our project is the translation and publication of the texts in the one hundred-volume Taishō edition of the Chinese Buddhist canon, along with a number of influential extracanonical Japanese Buddhist texts. The list of texts selected for the First Series of this translation project may be found at the end of each volume in the series.

As Chair of the Publication Committee, I am deeply honored to serve as the fifth person in a post previously held by leading figures in the field of Buddhist studies, most recently by my predecessor, John R. McRae.

In conclusion, I wish to thank the members of the Publication Committee for their dedicated and expert work undertaken in the course of preparing this volume for publication: Senior Editor Marianne Dresser, Dr. Hudaya Kandahjaya, Dr. Carl Bielefeldt, Dr. Robert Sharf, and Rev. Brian Kensho Nagata, Director of the BDK America English Tripiṭaka Project.

A. Charles Muller
Chairperson
Publication Committee

Contents

A Message on the Publication of the English Tripiṭaka
NUMATA Yehan v

Editorial Foreword *MAYEDA Sengaku* vii

Publisher's Foreword *A. Charles Muller* ix

Esoteric Texts

The Sutra of the Vow of Fulfilling the Great Perpetual Enjoyment and Benefiting All Sentient Beings Without Exception

Contents 3

Translator's Introduction 5

The Sutra of the Vow of Fulfilling the Great Perpetual Enjoyment and Benefiting All Sentient Beings Without Exception 9

Notes 25

The Mātaṅga Sutra

Contents 29

Translator's Introduction 31

The Mātaṅga Sutra 35

Notes 93

The Bodhicitta Śāstra

Contents 103

Translator's Introduction 105

The Bodhicitta Śāstra 107

Notes 129

Glossary 131

Bibliography 139

Index 141

A List of the Volumes of the BDK English Tripiṭaka (First Series) 151

THE SUTRA OF THE VOW OF FULFILLING THE GREAT PERPETUAL ENJOYMENT AND BENEFITING ALL SENTIENT BEINGS WITHOUT EXCEPTION

Contents

Translator's Introduction 5

The Sutra of the Vow of Fulfilling the Great Perpetual Enjoyment and Benefiting All Sentient Beings Without Exception

Introduction 11

1. The Way of Supreme Joy 11
2. The Way of Enlightenment 13
3. The Way of Conquest 14
4. The Way of Seeing the Self-nature 15
5. The Way of Discovering the Jewel 15
6. The Way of Karma 16
7. The Way of Turning the Wheel of a Letter (*Akṣara-cakra*) 17
8. The Way of Entering the Great Wheel (*Cakra*) 17
9. The Way of Worship 18
10. The Way of Wrath 19
11. The Way of Assembling the Vow (*Samaya*) 19
12. The Way of Empowerment 20
13. The Way of the Seven Heavenly Mothers 20
14. The Way of the Three Brothers 21
15. The Way of the Four Sisters 21
16. The Way of Perfection 21
17. The Way of the Mysteries 22

Concluding Prayer of Praise 23

Notes 25

Translator's Introduction

The *Prajñāpāramitānaya-*[*sūtra*] (Jp. *Hannyarishukyō*) (Taishō vol. 8, no. 243) consists of three sections: an introduction, the main body of the text, and a discourse in seventeen chapters (stages), ending with a concluding verse of praise. Each of the seventeen chapters of the discourse consists of three or four parts: an introductory message, the discourse, and its emphasis or religious merits, in which various esoteric symbols such as mantras, *mudrās*, seed syllables (*bīja*), and ritual implements are effectively expressed through a cosmological drama.

Throughout the chapters the importance of human nature, such as the emotions of craving, passion, desire, and anger, is exposed and emphasized as the chief force of enlightenment, leading one toward nirvana. Negative views of human nature, which often appear in other Buddhist schools and are common in other religions, are absent from this text. Instead of a negative view of human nature, the sutra provides a way of magnifying human awareness through which reality is apprehended and embodied. In this process of universalization, various symbols, including mantras, seed syllables, bodhisattvas, and *mudrās*, are effectively employed and arranged in seventeen stages to produce a cosmological, religious drama/activity. An ineffable esoteric experience of the Shingon tradition is well expressed and exposed in the particular encountering pattern in which Mahāvairocana Tathāgata changes his form in retinue.

More precisely, this literary work (*sūtra*) by an unknown seventh-century Indian Buddhist (or Buddhists) provides a religious pathway by which one may transcend human limitations and discover everlasting peace in this very life. Emphasizing the importance of human nature for enlightenment, it depicts an ideal being, Vajrasattva (Jp. Kongōsatta), in its universal drama. The title "The Way of Great Enjoyment" attributed to this sutra means the way of magnifying the scope of human craving or lust (using desire as an incentive), and it is precisely this magnification of desire that becomes the means of salvation.

This literal translation of this text is mainly based on the eighth-century Chinese version by Amoghavajra (Ch. Bukong), taking into consideration the Japanese version translated by Dr. Shōun Toganoo, a modern philologist and scholar in the Shingon Buddhist tradition. Several key terms and crucial words remain in their original Sanskrit in order to avoid further misinterpretation and distortion. My primary aim for this translation is to introduce the religious significance of the sutra to Westerners, considering the context and usage of this text in the modern Shingon tradition.

The *Hannyarishukyō* has been extensively used in the Japanese Shingon tradition, and is still recited daily by all Shingon monks and priests (including myself). Its ritual practice, the *Rishu-bō,* in the form of a *sādhana* (ritual formula to be performed for fulfillment), is performed daily for esoteric enlightenment and for many other purposes.

In the context of its use, every word, deity, mantra, *mudrā,* and seed syllable in the sutra is taken seriously as an important religious symbol that evokes or arouses the emotional motivation to transform one's human condition. The meaning of such esoteric symbols is repeatedly explained in the form of a dialogue between a preacher and his assembly/retinue throughout the discourse, emphasizing the way of transformation—the way of universalizing human nature.

The *Prajñāpāramitānaya-sūtra* was originally composed in Sanskrit sometime in the seventh century C.E. in India, and the text was introduced to China in the early part of the eighth century when the Indian Buddhist master Amoghavajra (705–774 C.E.), the fourth patriarchal master of the Esoteric Shingon tradition, translated it into Chinese in the capital city, Chang'an. The sutra recited by Shingon monks today is Amoghavajra's Chinese version. The full Sanskrit title of the sutra is *Mahāsukhavajra-amoghasamaya-sūtra* (Ch. *Dale jingang bukong zhenshi sanmohe jing*), referred to by Japanese monks by the abbreviated title *Hannyarishukyō* (Ch. *Banruo liqu jing*). Master Bukong also wrote a vast commentary on the sutra. In the early ninth century, Kōbō Daishi (Kūkai), the founder of Japanese Esoteric Buddhism, brought the text to Japan after his period of study in China. Since its introduction to Japan, the sutra has become the main textual source for esoteric rituals and served as the theoretical basis of Shingon teaching.

Dr. Toganoo made a great contribution by compiling a large commentary on the sutra, the *Rishukyō no kenkyū* (*A Study of the Rishukyō*) (Koyasan: Koyasan University Press, 1959), and in 1950 he completed a translation of the text into modern Japanese, *Wabun Kyōten: Hannyarishukyō* (*Hannyarishukyō in Modern Japanese*) (Koyasan: Koyasan Shuppansha, 1973, reprint).

I am not yet fully satisfied with my work here, leaving it to experts to explain in clear English the apparently unintelligible and the esoteric terms, so that the sutra can be understood by all.

For the preparation of this work, I wish to acknowledge my friend, Dr. Richard K. Payne of Los Gatos, California, who made corrections to my first draft. I completed this English translation in 2004, the year of the forty-fifth anniversary of my Buddhist mission in America, and I would like to express my sincere appreciation and gratitude to all the members of the Kōyasan Shingon Mission in Los Angeles for their support of my work and financial contribution, which made my Daishi mission possible.

Sutra of the Vow of Fulfilling the Great Perpetual Enjoyment and Benefiting All Sentient Beings Without Exception (*Mahāsukhavajra-amoghasamaya-sūtra*): *The Way of the Perfection of Wisdom* (*Prajñāpāramitānaya*)

Translated into Chinese by the Great Vast Wisdom in the Tripiṭaka, Śramaṇa Amoghavajra (Bukong) of Daxingshansi Temple, Chang'an, China, who received the honorary title of Governor General with Honorary Rank Equal to That of the Three Official Dignitaries in the Court; the Especially Advanced and [Appointed] Probationary Chief Minister of the Court of State Ceremonial; Duke of the Region of Su with a fief of three thousand households, upon whom was bestowed the purple robe; the [Judicial] Minister of the Civil and Land Services; and the posthumous title of Dazheng Jian.

Introduction

Thus have I heard: Thereupon, the Glorious One, Lord Vairocana, perfected the wisdom of excellent vow (*samaya*) of the imperishable empowerment 784a (*adhiṣṭhāna*) of all tathāgatas. After donning the empowered jeweled crown of all the tathāgatas he obtained mastery of the triple world.

Realizing the mastery in unhindered yoga with the wisdom of all wisdoms of all the tathāgatas, he equally performed all the various tasks and missions of the sameness of all the *mudrā*s of all the tathāgatas.

He totally fulfilled every wish of all sentient beings in the worlds without exception; continuously, through three generations and all times he had shown his perpetual [yet harmonious] acts of body, speech, and mind.

Mahāvairocana took up his abode in the heavenly pavilion Paranirmitavaśavartin, which still belongs to the realm of sense desire. This eternal pavilion of all the tathāgatas was an auspicious, praiseworthy palace made of great *maṇi* jewels. It was bedecked with various silk streamers with windbells, fluttering softly in the breezes, and decorated with strings of pearls, jeweled garlands, pendants, and hanging mirrors in the shapes of full and half-moons.

Vairocana Tathāgata dwelled together with eighty *koṭī* (eight billion) bodhisattvas, headed by Vajrapāṇi Bodhisattva-mahāsattva, Avalokiteśvara Bodhisattva-mahāsattva, Ākāśagarbha Bodhisattva-mahāsattva, Vajramusti Bodhisattva-mahāsattva, Mañjuśrī Bodhisattva-mahāsattva, Sacittotpādadharmacakrapravartin Bodhisattva-mahāsattva, Gaganagañja Bodhisattva-mahāsattva, and Sarvamārapramardin Bodhisattva-mahāsattva, and other great bodhisattvas.

Surrounded and accompanied by those bodhisattvas, he delivered the teaching (Dharma) that is lovely in the beginning, lovely in the middle, lovely in the end, well expressed, immaculate, perfect, and quite pure. 784b

[1. The Way of Supreme Joy]

At that time, the Glorious One, Lord Vairocana, turned the wheel of the Dharma here in making clear the principle that all *dharma*s are pure in their own being:

Enraptured and embraced in the heart of the Buddha,
Received in the grace of the compassion,
Enclosed in affection of the great, profound love,
One who knows the purity of the true state[1] of the self-nature is a bodhisattva (*surata*).[2]
An arrow of the craving and eager affection shot,
Quickly reaches and touches the beloved one.
Tied with the threads of immaculate love,
Live in joy and win the mastery of will.
One who knows the purity of such a state [of rapture] is a bodhisattva.

Seeing the Buddha as he is,
Delighting in touch with the beloved one,
Enlarging the scope of love,
Gained in heraldic dignity (dignitary pride),
One who knows the purity of such a state [of enjoyment] is a bodhisattva.

Donning/decorating with a flower garland,
Inspiring the great pleasure in mind (*āhlādana*),
Illuminating the light of compassion,
Rejoice in the physical pleasure.
One who knows the purity of such a state is a bodhisattva.

The color to be seen is Buddha,
The sound to be heard is his voice,
The odor to be smelled is the fragrance of his Dharma,
The taste to be touched is his teaching.
One who knows the purity of such a state [of sensory perception] is a bodhisattva.

And why? Because all *dharma*s (things) are pure in their own being. Accordingly, the *prajñāpāramitā* (perfection of wisdom) is pure and clean.

Vajrapāṇi! If anyone hears the way of perfection of wisdom that consummates the words of the purity of all *dharma*s in their own beings, until reaching at the *bodhi* seat, he will not fall into hell or on the way to hell even if he has accumulated all obstructions, such as the obstruction of defilements, the obstruction of *dharma*s, and the obstruction of karma.

And even when he commits serious sins, he is capable of eliminating them without difficulty. If he receives and holds, recites daily, thinks, and meditates [on this sutra], he will attain to the state of eternal *samādhi* of the equality of all *dharma*s in this very life, gain mastery of all *dharma*s, and receive immeasurable joy and pleasure. Moreover, with the sixteen great bodhisattvas' lives (merits) he will attain to the state of tathāgata and [that of] a *vajra*-holder bodhisattva.

At that time, Lord Vajrapāṇi, great bodhisattva, perfecter of all beneficial tasks, unexcelled conqueror of triple realm, excellent *vajra*-holder, who resides and dwells in all the *maṇḍala*s that reveal the vow of the enlightenment of the Great Vehicle of all the tathāgatas, wishing to show clearly this significance again, smiled softly and held the *mūdra* of immovable confidence with his left hand and tossed up the original great *vajra* implement (five-pronged *vajra*) in his right hand, forming the posture of courageous pride. Then he uttered the essence of the imperishable vow of fulfilling the great enjoyment/bliss and benefiting all beings without exception as *hūṃ*.[3]

[2. The Way of Enlightenment]

Thereupon, Lord Vairocana Tathāgata delivered the way of the perfection of wisdom that produces awakening to the sameness of the peaceful, calm Dharma-nature of all the tathāgatas.

Where one has awakened to the sameness of the imperishable nature of all being,
There is perfect enlightenment.
Because it is perpetually immovable and adamantine in its own being. (*vajra*) 784c

Where one has awakened to the sameness of the beneficial nature of existents,
There is great enlightenment.
Because it is beneficent in its own being. (*ratna*)

Where one has become aware of the sameness of the Dharma (teaching),
There is perfect enlightenment.
Because it is pure in its own-being. (*dharma*)

Where one has awakened to the sameness of karma (activities),
There is the perfect enlightenment.
Because it is nondiscrimination of all discriminated things. (karma)

Vajrapāṇi! If someone listens to this teaching of the four [major] producing *dharma*s, reads, receives, and holds it, even if in the present he immeasurably commits serious sins, he will surely be able to transcend all evil destinies and, seated on the *bodhi* seat, he will quickly realize unsurpassed enlightenment.

Then the Lord had thus delivered [this teaching]. In order to show clearly the significance [of the four phases of enlightenment] again, he smiled softly, held the *mudrā* of "wisdom fist," and manifested the essence of the sameness of the self-nature of all things as *āh.*[4]

[3. The Way of Conquest]

Thereupon, Śākyamuni Tathāgata, the conqueror/subduer of all evil enemies, delivered again the way of the perfection of wisdom that produces the supreme conquest of the sameness of all *dharma*s:

Because of the non-obsessed (*aprapañca*) nature of craving/greed,
Anger has non-obsessed nature.

Because of the non-obsessed nature of hate,
Folly has a non-obsessed nature.

Because of the non-obsessed nature of folly,
All things are of non-obsessed nature.

Because of the non-obsessed nature of all things, one should know
That *prajñāpāramitā* is of non-obsessed nature.

Vajrapāṇi! If anyone listens to this guiding principle and receives and holds it, then even when he harms all beings in the triple world he will not fall into evil destinies. Because he has subdued, he will immediately attain unsurpassed perfect enlightenment.

Then Vajrapāṇi, the great bodhisattva, wishing to clearly expound again this significance, held the *mudrā* of conquering the triple realm (*trailokyavijayarāja mudrā*) with a smiling lotus face, and frowned angrily and glared. Showing his

sharp fangs, he stayed in the standing pose of conquering and uttered the essence 785a
of the *vajra-hūṃ-kara* (wrathful mantra) as *hum.*[5]

[4. The Way of Seeing the Self-nature]

Thereupon, Lord Svabhāvaśuddha Tathāgata (Avalokiteśvara), who has embodied the nature of self-purity, delivered the way of the perfection of wisdom that explicates the seal of cognition, which is seeing skillfully the equality of all *dharmas*:

Because all worldly greed is purified,
All hatred is purified.

Because all worldly defilements are purified,
All sins are purified.

Because all worldly *dharmas* are purified,
All beings are purified.

Because the wisdom that comprehends all worldly phenomena
is purified,
Prajñāpāramitā is purified.

Vajrapāṇi! If someone listens to this way of the perfection of wisdom, reads, recites, thinks, and meditates on it, even if he abides in much craving, like a lotus he will not be stained by defilements and will quickly attain unsurpassed perfect enlightenment.

At that time, Lord Bodhisattva Avalokiteśvara, wishing again to expound clearly this meaning, smiled softly, formed a gesture of the opening lotus petals, and observed the nondefilement of desire. Then he uttered the essence of the various forms of all existents as *hrīh.*[6]

[5. The Way of Discovering the Jewel]

Thereupon, the Lord Tathāgata who has become the king of the entire triple world, again delivered the way of the perfection of wisdom that is called here the source of the consecrated wisdom of all the tathāgatas:

One who is empowered with the consecrating water
Becomes the king of the triple world.

One who receives the gift of benefiting
Fulfills all his wishes and hopes.

One who receives the gift of Dharma (the Buddha's teaching)
Awakens to the perfection of all Dharma-nature.

One who receives the requisites of life
Rejoices at all the peaceful pleasures of body, speech, and mind.

Then, the great bodhisattva Ākāśagarbha, wishing to expound this meaning again, smiled gently, place the jeweled *vajra* crown on his own head, and uttered the essence of the jewel of all consecrated vows as *trām.*[7]

[6. The Way of Karma]

Thereupon the Lord Tathāgata, who has held the seal of cognition [of the skillful activities] of all the tathāgatas, delivered the method of the perfection of wisdom that is called here the way of empowering acts of all the tathāgatas with the *mudrā* of cognition:

Holding the *mudrā* of the body of all the tathāgatas
Results in becoming the body of all the tathāgatas.

Holding the *mudrā* of the speech of all the tathāgatas
Results in attaining the teaching of all the tathāgatas.

Holding the *mudrā* of the mind of all the tathāgatas
Results in attaining the *samādhi* of all the tathāgatas.

Holding the *mudrā* of the *vajra* of all the tathāgatas
Results in the perfection of the supreme powers of
Body, speech, and mind of all the tathāgatas.

Vajrapāṇi! If someone listens to this guiding method, receives, recites, reflects on, and thinks it, he will not only gain all the masteries and the wisdom of knowledge of all phenomena but will also accomplish all activities and all perfections. Then he will succeed in gaining all the powers of the imperishable nature of all physical, verbal, and mental acts; [consequently,] he will quickly realize unsurpassed, perfect enlightenment.

Then Lord Great Bodhisattva Vajramuṣti delivered a *mudrā* to express the significance of this method again, smiled softly, and formed the *mudrā* of the *samaya vajra* fist in his hands. Then he exposed the true essence of the self that is the vow of the perfection of all the firm, indestructible *mudrās* as *aḥ*.[8]

[7. The Way of Turning the Wheel of a Letter (*Akṣara-cakra*)]

Thereupon, the Lord Tathāgata, who has liberated himself out of discursive, discriminatory knowledge, delivered the way of the perfection of wisdom that is called here the turning of the wheel of a letter (*akṣara-cakra*):

All things are empty, because of concomitance with
The absence of self-nature.

All things have nonappearance, because of concomitance
With the markless.

All things are unobtainable, because of concomitance
With the non-obtainable nature.

All things are radiant, because of the purity of *prajñāpāramitā*.

Then the youthful Mañjuśrī Bodhisattva, wishing to clearly deliver this significance again, smiled softly, and slashing all the tathāgatas with his own sword, uttered the most excellent essence of the *prajñāpāramitā* as 785b
am.[9]

[8. The Way of Entering the Great Wheel (*Cakra*)]

Thereupon, the Lord Tathāgata who resides in the world of the great wheel delivered the way of the perfection of wisdom that is called here entering the great wheel:

Entering the sameness of adamantine [nature] is
Entering the Dharma wheel of all the tathāgatas.

Entering the sameness of wealth is
Entering the wheel of the great bodhisattvas.

Entering the sameness of all *dharma*s is
Entering the wonderful Dharma wheel.

Entering the sameness of all actions is
Entering the wheel of all karmic acts.

Then, the great bodhisattva Sacittotpādadharmacakrapravartin, wishing to once again clearly demonstrate this significance, smiled softly and turned the *vajra* wheel, then delivered the essence of all the imperishable vows [of entering into the *vajra cakra*] as *hūṃ.*[10]

[9. The Way of Worship]

Thereupon, the Lord Tathāgata, who has held a bowl and performed the grand ritual of worship of all the tathāgatas, delivered the way of the perfection of wisdom through which the supremacy of worship is produced and assured.

Giving rise to the mind of enlightenment (*bodhicitta*) is
Extensively worshiping all the tathāgatas.

Salvation of all sentient beings is
Extensively worshiping all the tathāgatas.

Receiving and holding the wonderful sutra is
Extensively worshiping all the tathāgatas.

Receiving and maintaining, reading, writing, instructing others, copying,
Contemplating, practicing, and variously devoting to (worshiping) the *prajñāpāramitā* are greater worship to
All the tathāgatas.

Then, the great bodhisattva Gaganagañja, wishing to clearly expound this significance again, smiled gently and uttered all the imperishable essence of the vow of accomplishing all the karmic actions of the worship without fail as *oṃ.*[11]

[10. The Way of Wrath]

Thereupon, Lord Tathāgata [Sarvavinayasamartha], who has held the wisdom fists ("wrathful fists") of discipline, delivered again the way of the perfection of wisdom that is called here "source of the knowledge of wrath":

Because of the sameness of all sentient beings,
Wrath is sameness.

Because of the disciplining of all sentient beings,
Wrath is discipline.

Because of the Dharma-nature of all sentient beings,
Wrath is Dharma-nature.

Because of the *vajra*-nature of all sentient beings,
Wrath is adamantine in nature.

And why?
Because the disciplining of all sentient beings is for the purpose of enlightenment.

Then, in order to expound this meaning the great bodhisattva Sarvamārapramadin smiled softly, held the *vajra* fangs (wrathful fists) in the form of Vajrayakṣa, frightened all the tathāgatas, and uttered the essence of the great laughter of *vajra* fury as *hah*.[12] 785c

[11. The Way of Assembling the Vow (*Samaya*)]

Thereupon, the Lord Tathāgata who establishes the sameness of all *dharma*s again delivered the way of the perfection of wisdom that produces the supreme excellence of the vow of assembling the sameness of all *dharma*s:

Because all things have the nature of sameness,
Prajñāpāramitā has the nature of sameness.

Because of the beneficial nature of all things,
Prajñāpāramitā has the nature of benevolence.

Because of the Dharma-nature of all things,
Prajñāpāramitā has the Dharma-nature.

Because of the karmic nature of all things,
Prajñāpāramitā has the nature of karma.
So should it be understood.

Then Vajrapāṇi entered the *samādhi* of the vow of empowerment of all tathāgatas and bodhisattvas and uttered the essence of the vow of assembling all the teachings without exception as *hūṃ.*[13]

[12. The Way of Empowerment]

Thereupon, the Lord Tathāgata who consecrates all sentient beings delivered again the way of the perfection of wisdom that reveals that all sentient beings are capable of becoming a buddha with their own nature through his empowering activities:

All beings are the womb of the Tathāgata (*tathāgatagarbha*)
Because they store all with the self of Samantabhadra Bodhisattva.

All beings are the source of the imperishable nature (*vajra*)
Because they are consecrated by its power.

All beings are the source of the marvelous Dharma
Because they can turn it well to all words.

All beings are the source of activities
Because they correspond with the nature of creativity [by means of making the actions well].

Then the celestial deity [Maheśvara], who resides in the outer *cakra* of the *vajra* assembly, raised a clamor of self-satisfaction to show this significance again, and delivered the true essence of his own self of the perpetual mastery and sovereignty as *trī.*[14]

[13. The Way of the Seven Heavenly Mothers]

At that time, the Seven Deva Mothers knelt down at the foot of the Lord, paid homage to him, and offered the heart-mantra that produces the vow of hooking, guiding, destruction, and perfection as *bhyo.*[15]

[14. The Way of the Three Brothers]

At that time, the heavenly guardians the Three Brothers, including Madhukāra, knelt down together to the Lord, paid homage, and offered the heart-mantra *svā.*[16]

[15. The Way of the Four Sisters]

At that time, the heavenly guardians the Four Sisters [of Tumburu] offered the heart-mantra to the Lord as *ham.*[17]

[16. The Way of Perfection]

Thereupon, the Lord Tathāgata, who embodies the infinite, boundless, yet utmost nature of all *dharma*s, again delivered the way of the perfection of wisdom that produces the sameness and imperishability [of all the *dharma*s], in order to empower and ultimately perfect this teaching [mentioned above]:

Because *prajñāpāramitā* is immeasurable, all tathāgatas are
Immeasurable.

Because *prajñāpāramitā* is boundless, all tathāgatas are 786a
Boundless.

Because all things are of one nature, *prajñāpāramitā* is
Of one nature.

Because all things are ultimate, *prajñāpāramitā* is
Ultimate.

Vajrapāṇi! If someone listens to this guiding principle, receives and maintains it, reads it, and meditates on its meaning, he will complete the ultimate conduct in the practice of the Buddha and bodhisattvas.

[17. The Way of the Mysteries]

Thereupon, Lord Vairocana Tathāgata of non-obsession, who gained the secret nature of all *dharma*s, expounded again the way of the perfection of wisdom that is supreme, without beginning, middle, or end, and which has the imperishable Dharma-nature of the vow of fulfilling the great perpetual bliss and benefiting all beings without exception:

Bodhisattva-mahāsattva! Because of the supreme perfection of great craving (*rāga*),
One attains the supreme perfection of the great bliss.

Bodhisattva-mahāsattva! Because of the supreme perfection of great bliss,
One attains the supreme perfection of the great enlightenment of all the tathāgatas.

Bodhisattva-mahāsattva! Because of attaining the supreme perfection of all the tathāgata's great enlightenment,
One attains the supreme perfection of all the tathāgatas, which crushes the power of all demon Māras.

Bodhisattva-mahāsattva! Because of attaining the supreme perfection of all the tathāgatas, which cuts off the power of all demon Māras,
One attains the perfection of sovereign mastery of everywhere in the triple realm.

Bodhisattva-mahāsattva! Because of attaining the perfection of sovereign mastery of everywhere in the triple realm,
One purifies all beings in the world, without exception, abiding in transmigration.
Making great effort, he dwells in samsara the world of birth and death,
And accomplishes all the most excellent ultimate works that save, benefit, and bring peaceful joy to all.

And why?
Because:

Bodhisattvas of great knowledge,
Until the extinction of life and death
Constantly benefit sentient beings,
Without entering nirvana.

With wisdom and skillful means,
They completely empower and purify
All things and beings.

Subduing the world with desires,
Leads to the attainment of purification.
From the highest heaven to hell
They totally subdue all beings.

Like a lotus' original color
That cannot be stained by mud.
So also the nature of many desires does not stain beings;
Rather it benefits them.

Realizing the purity of great desire,
They have peaceful joy and great abundance.
Gaining mastery of the triple realm,
They steadily take on the mission of benefiting others.

Vajrapāṇi! If anyone hears this essential way of the perfection of wisdom, recites it early each morning, and listens to it [in mind], he will not only obtain all peaceful joys and pleasures but will also gain the ultimate perfection of the vow of fulfilling the great perpetual bliss and benefiting all beings without exception. In the present world he will obtain the blissful mastery of all *dharma*s, embodying the sixteen great bodhisattvas' lives 786b
(merits), and attain the state of [Mahāvairocana] Tathāgata and the *vajra*-holder bodhisattva [Vajradhara]."

Hūṃ![18]

[Concluding Prayer of Praise]

Thereupon, all the tathāgatas and *vajra*-holder bodhisattva-mahāsattvas came together and assembled, because they wished to quickly realize this teaching and make it a perfect, unhindered [Dharma] without exception. They all together praised Vajrapāṇi, saying:

Well done! Well done! Great Being Mahāsattva!
Fine! Fine! Great Peaceful Joy!
Splendid! Splendid! Great Vehicle!
Marvelous! Marvelous! Great Wisdom!

Well [Vajrapāṇi] has skillfully delivered this Dharma teaching,
and empowered this *vajra* sutra!
Those who hold this unsurpassed teaching cannot be destroyed
by the Māras.
They attain the highest state of the Buddha and bodhisattvas,
and are not long in accomplishing many *siddhi*s.
All the tathāgatas and bodhisattvas performed and accomplished
this excellent teaching.
In order to perfect quickly those who have held this teaching, everyone
[in the assembly] had great joy and faith, and received and practiced
[this teaching].

[End of the *Sutra of the Vow of Fulfilling the Great Perpetual Enjoyment and Benefiting All Sentient Beings Without Exception*]

Notes

[1] Translation of the Sanskrit *pāda,* which literally means "step, move on, footstep, pace." Here I have translated it as "state of" or "spiritual state of."

[2] This stanza is a poetic translation of the Sanskrit *surata,* pleasure or delightful ecstasy through sexual intercourse. It is used here as the symbolic expression of the great love in form of the mutual interaction, the union of rapture.

[3] Here the seed syllable *hūṃ* is attributed to the ideal eternal being Vajrasattva, who penetrates into the human body, evokes the mind of enlightenment, and pursues the way of salvation.

[4] The seed syllable *āh* denotes four major phases of enlightenment—imperishable, beneficial, purity, and nondiscriminating action—and is used here as the identifying symbol of Mahāvairocana Buddha.

[5] The seed syllable *hum* refers to a furious angry voice, an interjection.

[6] The seed syllable *hrīh* is widely used in the Shingon tradition to identify Avalokiteśvara, Amitābha, and Amitāyus as symbols of self-purity and compassion.

[7] The syllable *trām* is the symbol of Ākāśagarbha Bodhisattva and corresponds to the nature of benefiting and meritorious gifts.

[8] The seed syllable *aḥ* symbolizes the nonabiding state of nirvana. It also corresponds to the nature of salvation as giving up one's own merit and dedicating it to others for their benefit.

[9] Normally the seed syllable *aṃ* refers to the initial vow of Mañjuśrī. It should be understood here as the symbol of transcending to enlightenment through nondiscriminating knowledge.

[10] Here *hūṃ* is a joyous interjection made upon entering into the *cakra.*

[11] In the Esoteric Buddhist tradition the syllable *oṃ* is used as a mantra in rites for offering and devoting worship to the deity that is to be identified with a practitioner.

[12] According to Amoghavajra's description in his commentary, this mantra is explained as the symbol of an imperishable yet wrathful activity in the nonabiding state of nirvana. It is the identifying symbol of Vajrayakṣa.

[13] The seed syllable *hūṃ* signifies the means of assembling, collecting, and condensing.

[14] The seed syllable *trī* means converting all sentient beings into the world of the Buddha, the non-arising realm.

[15] The word *bhyo* is attributed here to the *mudrā* of *vajra*-hooking and signifies turning all sentient beings to the buddha vehicle.

[16] The seed syllable *svā* signifies that all of the Three Brothers are real appearances of the unspeakable, ineffable, truthlike space.

[17] The syllable *ham* indicates that the Four Sisters are released from their harmful activities, causing their self-existing characters to vanish and their attainment of enlightenment.

[18] The seed syllable *hūṃ* here is the identifying symbol of Vajrasattva, who interiorizes himself in every human body. It refers to the totality of all four natures of Vajrasattva.

THE MĀTAṄGA SUTRA

Contents

Translator's Introduction 31

The Mātaṅga Sutra

Fascicle One

Chapter I. The Conversion of Prakṛti 37

Chapter II. Clarifying Past Connections 45

Chapter III. Revealing the Truth 55

Chapter IV. Questions 57

Chapter V. Explaining the Star Charts 61

Fascicle Two

Chapter VI. Observing Misfortune and Good Fortune 67

Chapter VII. Clarifying Distinctions of Time 85

Notes 93

Translator's Introduction

The *Mātaṅga Sutra* (Taishō vol. 21, no. 1300) is said to have been translated in 230 C.E. by Zhu Lüyan, an Indian monk, and Zhi Qian, a layman of Indo-Scythian origin, in Yangdu, the capital of the kingdom of Wu. This would make it the earlier of two Chinese versions of the Sanskrit *Śārdūlakarṇāvadāna,* which is included in the *Divyāvadāna,* a fourth-century collection of biographical narratives (*avadāna*). The second Chinese version (Taishō no. 1301) was translated by Dharmarakṣa during the Yongjia era (307–313) of the Western Jin (265–316), and in addition there are two Chinese translations of the frame story, one (Taishō no. 551) attributed to An Shigao (fl. ca. 148–180 C.E.) and the other (Taishō no. 552) by an unknown translator of the Eastern Jin (317–420).

It should be noted, however, that the traditionally accepted sequence of these four Chinese translations—Taishō nos. 551, 552, 1300, and 1301—has been questioned by the Japanese scholar Tomojirō Hayashiya, who established a quite different sequence on the basis of careful scrutiny of the vocabulary of the translations and early Chinese scriptural inventories. According to Hayashiya, the four Chinese versions were translated in the following order: Taishō no. 1301 (translated by Dharmarakṣa), no. 551, no. 552 (both translated by unknown translators during the Western Jin or earlier), and no. 1300 (translated by an unknown translator in the second half of the fifth century or later). This would mean that the version here translated into English is in fact the latest of the four Chinese versions.

Be that as it may, there is also a Tibetan translation from the mid-ninth century (Peking no. 1027, Derge no. 358), and variations of the frame story are found in other works too; it provides, for example, the occasion for the exposition of the *Śūraṅgama-sūtra* (Taishō no. 945). It is perhaps hardly surprising that this story should have been so popular, concerning as it does the love of Prakṛti, an outcaste girl, for the Buddha's renowned disciple Ānanda. In more modern times this same tale provided the plot for one of Richard Wagner's uncompleted works, an opera that was to be called *Die Sieger* (*The Victors*), and Rabindranath Tagore's play *Chandalika* is likewise based on this story.

According to our text, Prakṛti, a member of the outcaste *caṇḍālas*, fell in love with Ānanda after he asked her for a drink of water one day when he was returning from the city of Śrāvastī, where he had gone to beg for alms. With the help of her mother, a great sorceress who casts a spell on Ānanda, Prakṛti succeeds in drawing Ānanda to her home, but Ānanda is saved from his predicament by the miraculous intervention of the Buddha, and Prakṛti eventually becomes a nun. However, the ordination of an outcaste woman causes consternation among the citizens of Śrāvastī and they report the matter to King Prasenajit. The king then visits the Buddha, who proceeds to relate to the assembled multitude the story of a past life of the nun Prakṛti, a story that concerns Triśaṅku, king of the outcaste Mātaṅgas, who wished to marry his son Śārdūlakarṇa to the daughter (Prakṛti by name) of a brahman called Puṣkarasārin. At first Puṣkarasārin angrily rejects Triśaṅku's overtures, but in the course of a lengthy discussion between the two men Puṣkarasārin becomes convinced of Triśaṅku's learning and eventually gives his consent to the marriage of his daughter to Śārdūlakarṇa. It turns out that in a former life the Buddha himself was Triśaṅku, Ānanda was Śārdūlakarṇa, Śāriputra was Puṣkarasārin, and Puṣkarasārin's daughter Prakṛti was the nun of the same name. This work is thus a typical *avadāna,* consisting of a story set in the present (i.e., the story of Ānanda and Prakṛti); a story set in the past, explaining the karmic background to present circumstances; and a final resolution in which the Buddha clarifies the links between people in the past and people in the present.

The discussion between Triśaṅku and Puṣkarasārin accounts for the greater part of the text and traverses a wide range of topics. Of particular interest is the trenchant critique of the caste system, but considerable space is also devoted to astronomical and astrological lore, especially in regard to the twenty-eight "lunar mansions" (*nakṣatra*), corresponding to the twenty-eight divisions of the sky, each identified by a prominent star or asterism, through which the moon passes during its monthly cycle. Further topics covered include various units of time, weights and measures, intercalation, and physiognomy. The extant Sanskrit text includes additional chapters on various arts of prognostication and so on found in neither the Chinese nor Tibetan translations, suggesting that these chapters were added at a later date.

While most of the content of the Sanskrit text (apart from these additional chapters) is covered in the Chinese version translated here, there are considerable differences in the ordering of the subjects treated. (In contrast, the other Chinese translation, by Dharmarakṣa, generally follows the order of the Sanskrit text but omits several sections.) It is also evident that when translating passages dealing with astronomy the Chinese translators did not necessarily follow the original text faithfully but modified it on the basis of their own knowledge or observations. Some of the resulting discrepancies between the Sanskrit text and the Chinese translation, which are of some interest to historians of astronomy, have been mentioned briefly in the notes, but a more detailed discussion of these matters would go far beyond the scope of the present translation.

Lastly, it should be pointed out that the Chinese title of this text has in the past generally been rendered as *Mātaṅgī-sūtra* or *Sutra of the Mātaṅgī Girl,* "Mātaṅgī" being the feminine form of Mātaṅga, a member of a certain hill tribe and, by extension, an outcaste. This rendering has no doubt been influenced at least in part by the two Chinese translations of the frame story about Ānanda and Prakṛti, the titles of both of which refer to a "Mātaṅ[gī] Girl." But in the present case, the Chinese transcription points to "Mātaṅga" rather than "Mātaṅgī," and the title has therefore been rendered as *The Mātaṅga Sutra.* In the Chinese translation the designation "Mātaṅga" is reserved for the Mātaṅga king Triśaṅku, but in the Sanskrit *Śārdūlakarṇāvadāna* Prakṛti is called first a "Mātaṅga girl" and then a "*caṇḍāla* girl." Therefore, "Mātaṅga" in the title could refer either to the Mātaṅga king Triśaṅku, who is the central figure in the text, or to the nun Prakṛti, whose past circumstances the main story is meant to explain, or it could possibly encompass both.

The Mātaṅga Sutra

Translated by the Indian Tripiṭaka Master Zhu Lüyan
together with Zhi Qian in Wu

Fascicle One

Chapter I

The Conversion of Prakṛti

Thus have I heard. At one time the Buddha was staying in Anāthapiṇḍada's Garden in Jeta's Grove in the land of Śrāvastī, surrounded by monks and preaching the Dharma.

One morning the venerable Ānanda donned his robes, took his almsbowl, 400a
and entered the city [of Śrāvastī] to beg for food. Having finished begging for alms, he returned to Jeta's Grove. On the way there was a large pond where villagers gathered. Beside the pond was a woman of the *caṇḍāla* class carrying a pitcher who had just arrived to fetch water.[1] The elder Ānanda went up to where she was and said, "Sister, I am now thirsty and would very much like something to drink. Could you give me a little water?"

Thereupon the charitable woman said, "Virtuous sir, it's not that I'm stingy, but I am a *caṇḍāla* woman, and I fear that it would not be proper were I to offer you [water]."

Ānanda said, "Sister, I am a *śramaṇa* whose mind is impartial. I do not see any difference between the high and the low. Just give me [some water], for I should not linger." The woman then gave Ānanda some clean water, and when he had drunk it, he returned to his lodgings.

After he had left, the woman, seizing on Ānanda's countenance, voice, speech, deportment, and other attributes, engendered deep attachment and thoughts of desire flared up. She thought, "Wouldn't it be nice if I could get that departing monk to become my husband?" She further thought, "My mother is skilled in spells. She may be able to make him come to be my husband. I shall go to my mother and tell her all about it."

Then she took some water and returned home. She went to where her mother was and said, "[There is] a monk [called] Ānanda, who is a disciple of the Buddha. I am very much in love with him and want to win him as my husband. With the like of Mother's powers it should be possible to achieve this. Please take pity on me and fulfill my wish!"

Her mother said to her, "There are two kinds of people against whom it is of no avail to use magic. Who are those two? One is those who have cut off desire, and the second is the dead. Others I am able to subjugate. The *śramaṇa* Gautama is exalted in his awe-inspiring virtue, and King Prasenajit has great faith and respect for him. Were he to find out that I had made Ānanda come [here], the *caṇḍāla*s would all be annihilated. Furthermore, Gautama has extinguished mental afflictions, and his followers are all free from the defilement of desire. I once heard that to those who have cut off birth and death one should offer respect. Why would one instead commit evil deeds against them?"

When [her daughter] heard this, she wept with grief and said, "Mother, if you cannot make Ānanda come, I will most certainly forsake life and limb. Even if Gautama defies my wish, again I shall not be able to remain long in the world. If I win him (i.e., Ānanda), all my wishes will be fulfilled."

On hearing these words, her mother, saddened and unhappy, addressed her, saying, "You must not give up your life. I will assuredly be able to make Ānanda come here."

Thereupon the girl's mother smeared the ground in [the yard of] her home with cowdung, spread out reeds, and in the center of this site lit a great raging fire. [Taking] one hundred and eight fine *arka* flowers, she recited a spell
400b once for each flower and threw it into the fire. The spell said:

> *Amale vimale kuṅkume sumane, yena baddho 'si vidyut, icchayā devo varṣati vidyotati gajati vismaya[ṃ] ma[hā]rāja[sya] samabhivardhāyitum.*[2] (O you who are untainted, free from taint, saffron, and beautiful! O lightning, by which you are bound! According to desire the god rains down, flashes forth, and thunders to increase the amazement of the great king.)
>
> Gods and demons and *gandharva*s, the god of fire and the god of the earth—if you hear this spell of mine and my sacrifice, you should quickly make Ānanda come here!

When she had finished speaking these words, the venerable Ānanda immediately became confused in mind and, unaware of what he was doing, went to pay a visit to the *caṇḍāla*s' house.

Then the girl's mother, seeing Ānanda from afar approaching in a leisurely manner, addressed her daughter, saying, "The monk Ānanda has come and is drawing near. You should now lay out the bedding, burn incense, scatter flowers, and make everything very neat and clean."

On hearing her mother's words, the girl rejoiced and leapt for joy. She decorated the room, installed a bejeweled seat, cleaned [the room], sprinkled and swept [the floor], and scattered famed flowers.

By then Ānanda had already arrived at their house, sobbing with grief and choking, and he tearfully said, "How hapless I am to have met with this trouble! Could the World-honored One, with his great compassion, not take pity, apply his might, and think protectively of me so that I may be neither troubled nor harmed?"

Just then the Tathāgata saw with his pure divine vision that Ānanda was being led astray and confused by that woman, and in order to protect him he uttered a spell:

Sthiti acyuti anīti.[3]

Then the World-honored One, having uttered this spell, spoke these words: "With this spell I make all frightened beings feel at peace, and I also wish to bring benefit and ease to those in distress. Should there be any beings without a place of refuge, I shall become a true refuge for them." Thereupon the World-honored One further uttered these verses:

The pond of precepts is fresh and cool, clear and unsullied,
And it is able to lave the heat of the mental afflictions of beings.
Should any wise person enter this pond,
The obstacles of the darkness of ignorance will be completely
extinguished forever.
For this reason the worthies and sages of the three ages
All receive [the precepts] respectfully, and together they extol them.
If I have truly bathed in this stream,
It should make my attendant quickly return.

Then, because of the supernatural power of the Buddha and the power of his roots of goodness, the *caṇḍāla* spell had no effect on Ānanda, and he left their house and returned to Jeta's Grove. The girl saw Ānanda going back and said to her mother, "The monk has left!"

The mother addressed her, saying, "The *śramaṇa* Gautama is surely with his awesome power thinking protectively of him, and therefore he has been able to render my spell impotent."

400c The girl said to her mother, "Is the power of the supernatural virtues of the *śramaṇa* Gautama able to prevail over Mother?"

Her mother told her, "The virtues of the *śramaṇa* Gautama are profound and vast, and my power cannot be compared with his. Any magical arts of beings throughout the entire world he could, were he so disposed, destroy completely without there ever remaining anything of them. His actions cannot be hindered. For this reason know that his power is unsurpassed."

Around that [same] time Ānanda went to where the Buddha was, bowed down with his head at his feet, and stood to one side. The Buddha addressed Ānanda: "There is a six-phrase spell,[4] the power of which is preeminent: it completely protects all beings, destroys evil paths, and puts an end to calamities. You should now receive and uphold it, read and recite it, and use it for your own benefit and to make others happy. If monks, nuns, laymen, and laywomen wish to bring benefit and ease to themselves and to confer benefits on [other] beings, they should all receive and uphold the six-phrase divine spell. Ānanda, this entire spell was proclaimed by all six buddhas of the past, and now I, Śākyamuni Samyaksambuddha, also teach this spell. The heavenly king Great Brahmā, Śakra Devendra, the Four Heavenly Kings, and so on all revere it, receive and uphold it, and read and recite it. Therefore, you should now endeavor to practice, extol, and worship it without forgetting it." He then uttered the spell:

Yad uta, aṇḍare pāṇḍare keyūre [s]thāmihaste saragrīve bandhumati dharaviṣa cili mili bhanilinda yathā sambhakto lapolapati ka[ṇ]ṭhavilāya.[5]

The Buddha addressed Ānanda: "Should any being receive and uphold this six-phrase divine spell, then when he is about to be executed, he will through the power of the spell be lightly whipped and gain release; if he deserves a whipping, he will because of this spell escape with a reprimand;

and if he deserves a reprimand, he will on account of the awesome power of this divine spell be forever uncensured, calm and happy. Ānanda, I do not see any *śramaṇa,* brahman or god, demon, [denizen of the world of] Brahmā, human and non-human receiving and upholding this spell and then being troubled and harmed, except for those whose karma is fixed, about which nothing can be done."

Then the *caṇḍāla* girl, having passed the night, bathed herself, donned new and clean clothes, placed a garland of flowers on her head, applied perfume, adorned her person with gold and silver brooches and strings of pearls and, walking slowly at a leisurely pace, set out for the land of Śrāvastī. When she arrived at the city gate, she stood waiting for Ānanda.

That morning Ānanda entered the city to beg for food. The girl, seeing him coming, felt deep joy and went after him, never once leaving him. Whenever 401a
he stopped or moved on and whenever he entered [a house for alms] or came out, she always followed him. The venerable Ānanda, seeing this, felt greatly ashamed and, depressed and unhappy, he left the city and went to Jeta's Grove. He bowed down with his head at the Buddha's feet, withdrew, sat down to one side, and said to the Buddha, "World-honored One, [this] *caṇḍāla* girl is harassing me a great deal. Whether I go or stay, move or halt, she does not leave me. I but beg you, World-honored One, to extend protection out of compassion."

The Buddha addressed Ānanda: "You must not worry. I shall see to it that you are freed from this predicament."

Then the Buddha and World-honored One addressed the girl, saying, "Do you want Ānanda to be your husband?"

She said, "Gautama, it is truly as you say."

The Buddha said, "Good woman, the rules for marriage are such that one must tell one's parents. Have you now asked your honored [parents] or not?"

She replied, "Gautama, my parents have given me permission. Therefore I have come here."

The Buddha said, "If your parents have already granted permission, you must have them come themselves and hand you over in my presence."

On hearing these words, the girl bowed to the Buddha, withdrew, and set out for her parents' place. Having paid her respects, she withdrew and stood to one side, and said to her parents, "I want Ānanda to be my husband. Please have pity and go together with me to hand me over to him in person."

At this her parents made their way to where the Buddha was, bowed down with their heads at the Buddha's feet, and sat down to one side. The girl said, "Gautama, my parents have come."

Thereupon the World-honored One asked them, "Do you truly give your daughter to Ānanda?"

They replied, "World-honored One, it is indeed as you say."

The Buddha said, "You may now return to your dwelling place."

The girl's parents then bowed to the Buddha and withdrew, whereupon the Tathāgata addressed the girl, saying, "If you wish to win the monk Ānanda as your husband, you must leave home and assume his appearance."

She replied, "Yes, I shall respectfully accept your instructions."

The Buddha said, "Welcome!" whereupon she became a *śramaṇā,* and her hair fell away of its own accord and religious robes appeared on her person. Then [the Buddha] preached the Dharma for her, revealing and teaching it and benefiting and delighting her: namely, the discourse on giving, the discourse on the precepts, the discourse on birth in heaven, and that desire is impure and escape [from transmigration] is best. Further, this desire is an aggregation of sufferings, the palatability of which is very slight and the faults most plentiful. For example, just as moths out of ignorance throw themselves into blazing flames and burn themselves to death, so too ordinary people, with their inverted views, wrongly produce attachment and are impelled by craving, just like moths chasing flames. Therefore, the wise reject it and distance themselves from it, without for even a moment arousing thoughts of love.

Then, having heard [the Buddha] explain this, the nun was happy, rejoicing in her heart, and her mind became disciplined. Thereupon the World-honored One, knowing that the nun's heart and mind were pliant and free from troublesome hindrances, explained for her in full the Dharma of the four truths, that is, "This is suffering, this is the habituation of suffering, this is the cessation of suffering, and this is the path to the cessation of suffering."

401b Then the nun suddenly understood in her mind the four noble truths just as, for example, a new, clean, white cloth readily receives dye, and right there where she was sitting she attained the way of the arhat, never again to turn back or follow another's teaching. She bowed down with her head at the Buddha's feet and said to the Buddha, "World-honored One, earlier I was foolish. Intoxicated with the wine of desire, I upset a wise and holy person and created unwholesome karma. I but pray, World-honored One, that you will accept my confession."

The Buddha said, "I have already accepted your confession. You should now know that a buddha age (when a buddha is on earth) is difficult to encounter, a human body is difficult to obtain, and to be liberated from birth and death and gain [the state of] an arhat is also extremely difficult. These difficult things you have already accomplished, and in the Buddha's Dharma you have attained the fruit of truth. That is to say, birth and death have come to an end, pure conduct has been established, what had to be done has been done, and there will be no future existence for you. Therefore, you should now exert yourself, and be sure not to be negligent!"

Chapter II

Clarifying Past Connections

At that time the brahmans and eminent and ordinary householders in the city, hearing that the Buddha had converted a *caṇḍāla* woman and sent her forth from home on the path, were all outraged and said, "She is of a lowly class. How will she practice pure conduct together with the four groups [of practitioners]? How will she enter the homes of distinguished people to receive offerings?" In this fashion they discussed the matter in turn, and they also reported it to King Prasenajit. On hearing about it the king was greatly astonished, and he promptly prepared a carriage and, surrounded by retainers and with attendants preceding and following him, made his way to Jeta's Grove. There he alighted from the carriage, put aside his parasol, advanced slowly on foot, bowed down with his head at the Buddha's feet, withdrew, and sat down to one side.

The Buddha, knowing what was on the minds of those assembled and wishing to resolve their doubts, addressed the monks: "Do you wish to hear about the past circumstances of the nun Prakṛti (Original Nature) or not?"

The monks said, "Yes, we wish to hear about them."

"Listen carefully now, and I shall explain them for you.

"O monks, in time past, *asaṃkhyeya* (incalculable) eons ago, there was beside the Ganges River a garden called Atimukta in which flowers and fruits flourished and there were ponds and streams. In the garden there was a king by the name of Triśaṅku, who was of the *caṇḍāla-mātaṅga* class. He lived in this garden together with hundreds of thousands of myriads of *caṇḍāla*s.

"O monks, this Triśaṅku possessed great wisdom, was highly gifted and courageous, and knew his former lives, and there was nothing in the affairs of the world that he had not mastered. I shall briefly describe his five virtues. First, he was thoroughly trained in the essentials of the secrets of the four Vedic canons, and there was nothing that he did not understand about them. Second, he was well versed in poetry and prose and in phraseology long and short. Third, he knew all about treatises, scriptures, and annals and had gone beyond sound to the other shore. Fourth, he was well versed in worldly sacrifices, magical arts, and medicine. Fifth, he was able to differentiate the marks of a great man. This wisdom of his was inexhaustible.

401c "This king had a son called Śārdūlakarṇa (Lion's Ear).[6] He was of handsome features, his practice of the precepts was pure, his mind was pliant, he was benevolent and gentle, he was looked up to by all on account of his virtues, and he was a pleasure to behold. The Mātaṅga king had instructed his son extensively in the classics and the magical arts, teaching him everything that he himself knew. Consequently Śārdūlakarṇa's knowledge was profound, just like his father's, the same and no different.

"As King Triśaṅku was lying in bed one night a thought suddenly occurred to him: 'My son is most outstanding in appearance, he is endowed with many virtues, people look up to him with respect, he is slowly growing up, and it is proper that he be betrothed. I must choose a comely fine match of surpassing talent and virtue, just like my son, and then I shall seek her for him.'

"At that time there was a brahman called Puṣkarasārin (Lotus-flower Essence). His lineage was prestigious, his parents were true-bred, for seven generations [the family line] had been pure and without miscegenation, and he was versed in the four Vedas, with few able to match him in talent and skill. There was at the time a king called Agnidatta (Fire-given)[7] who ruled over everything under the heavens, freely wielding his awesome power, and he had enfeoffed [Puṣkarasārin] with a settlement, giving him control over it, its land fertile and the people prosperous. The daughter of this Puṣkarasārin was called Prakṛti, and she was of outstanding virtue and appearance, just like Śārdūlakarṇa.

"King Triśaṅku formed this thought: 'Only Puṣkarasārin's daughter is especially wonderful. I shall seek her betrothal to my son.' Having formed this thought, early the following morning he mounted a large bejeweled carriage drawn by a team of four white horses and, surrounded in front and behind by a multitude of *caṇḍāla*s, left home, proceeding north, and headed toward that country [where Puṣkarasārin lived].

"Now, to the south of where Puṣkarasārin lived there was a park, called Sumanaska (Happy). Flowers and fruits thrived, trees grew luxuriantly, springs and bathing pools were filled to the brim with clean water, and different kinds of birds cavorted above, their doleful[8] sounds harmonious and a delight to hear. The park was vast, and in its agreeableness it was like the garden Nanda[na] of the gods.[9] The Mātaṅga king went into the park and waited for Puṣkarasārin.

"Now, that morning the brahman too [had mounted] a carriage drawn by a team of four white horses and, together with five hundred brahmans and surrounded by attendants, went to the park on an excursion. Along the way, the brahman instructed his disciples in matters like the arts, as well as performing recitation, and so arrived at the park.

"On seeing Puṣkarasārin approaching in a leisurely manner and with exceptional dignity, King Triśaṅku rejoiced in his heart and praised him in verse:

Like the sun when it first appears, its rays of light shining brightly,
So too is your awesome dignity, great sir.
Just as the drug from the Snowy Mountains (Himalayas) is preeminent among all drugs,
You, good sir, are exalted and unparalleled. 402a
The power of your virtues is sublime and most impressive,
Just like the autumn moon, supreme among the stars.
Like Brahmā, king of the gods, your wisdom is transcendent,
And all the gods look up to you.
Like Śakra Devendra, you are revered by all,
Extraordinarily handsome and incomparable.
I have extolled your merits but in brief;
Were one to describe them in full, one would be unable to exhaust them.

"Having spoken these verses, [Triśaṅku] rose and went to meet [Puṣkarasārin]. They further exchanged greetings and then sat down.

"Puṣkarasārin said, 'You are a *caṇḍāla,* the lowliest of the low, and yet you have come here. What do you want?'

"[Triśaṅku] replied, 'Good sir, there are in the world four things that one should practice. What are those four? First, the things that one has formerly done one remembers and does not forget. Second, one should bring benefit and ease to oneself. Third, one confers benefits on all beings. Fourth, one undertakes the act of marriage. For this reason I have now purposely come to visit you. I have a son called Śārdūlakarṇa whose looks are imposing and wisdom sublime, and he wishes to be betrothed. Your daughter is supremely wise, and in their minds they long very much for each other. I wish to ask for your daughter in marriage. Please be so kind as to give it your consideration and grant permission.'

"When Puṣkarasārin heard these words, the poison of anger flared up and he became extremely enraged, his face drawn tight, and frowning he spoke to him, saying, 'The Mātaṅga class is despised by people and is to be much feared and loathed, like poison and fire. I, now, am of the brahman caste, distinguished and respectable, and there is none better. I have mastered the Vedas and my wisdom is unparalleled. Why do you now want to come and insult me? Just as those with eyes all know the difference between the moon in the sky and the light of a firefly lamp, so too is the *caṇḍāla* class when compared with the brahman, the one respectable and the other inferior. You, now, are foolish and do not recognize [this difference between] high and low, and you have engendered in your mind aspirations for that which you cannot seek. You, a *caṇḍāla,* have those of your own kind [whom your son can marry]. Why do you want to defile a person of supreme purity? Further, if a brahman is imperfect in his practice of the precepts and unable to master the wonderful canon of the Vedas, [other] brahmans do not associate with him. How much more so in the case of a boorish fellow like you who has formed this idea! You should leave straightaway, and you ought not to linger lest outsiders hear of this strange talk!'

"Then Triśaṅku, having heard this, said, 'Good sir, I know all about the differences between high and low, that gold and jade are rare while earth and wood are base. But I do not now see that there is any difference between brahmans and *caṇḍāla*s, for you brahmans do not appear out of the sky while
402b the *caṇḍāla* class alone is born from the earth. Brahmans come into being through the womb, and so does the *caṇḍāla* class. You say that you are special, but this cannot be so. The death of a brahman is feared and abhorred by people, nor does anyone wish to see the death of a *caṇḍāla.* If you say that there are distinctions between high and low, why are there no differences in their birth and death?

"'In your view, it should be regarded that *caṇḍāla*s do wicked things, that they are violent and murderous, that they deceive beings, that they have no thoughts of compassion, and that for these reasons they are called lowly. I shall now explain all the evil deeds and false things concerning you brahmans. You institute lawsuits, you upset the wise and good, you conjure up ghosts, you read the stars and observe the moon, you join battle, and you kill beings. To put it briefly, everything evil is all the doing of brahmans.

"'You brahmans are by nature fond of delicacies, and you make the following statement: "If one offers a sacrifice, chanting a spell over a sheep and killing it, the sheep will without fail be born in heaven." If it were the case that [a sheep] would be born in heaven upon having had a spell chanted over it, why, now, do you not chant a spell over your own person, kill yourself in sacrifice, and seek birth in heaven? Why do you not chant spells over your parents, acquaintances, wife and children, and attendants, slay them all, and cause them to be born in heaven? That you do not destroy your own person and only kill sheep is, it should be known, all because brahmans want to eat meat. You falsely give such explanations to deceive people, and to say that you are superior is quite unwarrantable.

"'In brahmanic law one is called heinous and is not a brahman if one commits four kinds of offenses. What are [the] four? The first is killing brahmans, the second is committing adultery with one's teacher's wife, the third is stealing gold, and the fourth is drinking liquor. Only these four evils are called offenses. There is no retribution for any other killing. In your laws one is guilty of the offense of killing on account of having terminated another's life. If one kills other people [apart from brahmans], it is also called terminating life. Why is killing them not an offense for you [brahmans] alone? It is also the same with [the other offenses down to] drinking liquor.

"'Know that you [brahmans] are foolish and ignorant, perversely producing deluded thoughts. One cannot call this distinguished. Furthermore, a brahman who has committed the previous four offenses can still win absolution if he sincerely repents, holding the foot of a bedstead in his hand, wearing tattered robes, and hanging a human skull on his head.[10] If he repents thus for a full twelve years, his precepts will once again be complete and he will become a brahman. Such foolishness is concordant with erroneous views, and yet you engender arrogance, calling yourself distinguished. If one looks at it on this basis, the castes are all equal, and you should give your daughter to my son.'

"When Puṣkarasārin heard these words, his anger doubled and he said to Triśaṅku, 'You rashly make these statements without thinking. As a king, you should know three laws. The first is the law of the land, the second is the law of high and low, and the third is the law of taxes. There are four castes
402c in the world. They were all born from Brahmā. Brahmans were born from Brahmā's mouth, *kṣatriya*s were born from his shoulders, *vaiśya*s were born from his navel, and *śūdra*s were born from his feet.[11] It is because of this meaning that brahmans are deemed to be preeminent. They can have four wives, *kṣatriya*s three wives, *vaiśya*s two wives, and *śūdra*s one wife. Differentiated in this manner, the castes are each different. You yourself are so lowly that you do not even come within these four castes, and yet you say that there are no differences between the castes. This is contrary to the sacred teachings, and you want to confuse me. You should promptly go back home. Say no more!'

"Triśaṅku said, 'If, good sir, you say that the four castes in the world were all born from Brahmā and that brahmans alone came forth from his mouth, on account of which they are the most honorable and there are none better than them, then why do brahmans have hands, feet and joints, as well as the four kinds of deportment (walking, standing, sitting, and lying down) and voice and speech? For this reason know that there are no differences [between the castes]. Supposing that they did differ, you would have to distinguish between them. For example, there are various distinctions among lotuses, namely, flowers that grow in water or on land, the *utpala* flower, the fragrant *campaka* flower, the *atimuktaka* flower, and the *sumanā* flower. Flowers such as these have differences of color, and their fragrance also differs. But I do not see any differences in your four castes. You should realize that they are all distinctions of wrong thinking.

"'For example, a young child playing on the road gathers together sandy soil to make castles, or else he names [the grains of sand], saying, "This is gold, this is silver, ghee, curds, rice, wheat." But the sandy soil does not turn into rare treasures on account of the child's giving it names. In this fashion you too, your mind shrouded with foolishness, give rise to thoughts of arrogance. Nobility and lowliness do not come about just because you say so.

"'Again, if brahmans were born from the mouth of Brahmā, they ought to have compassion, tolerance, benevolence, and love for beings. How could they kill them, put curses on them, and be angry with them? Supposing that the four castes were all born from Brahmā, they would then be siblings. How could they undertake the act of marriage together? This would muddy propriety, run counter to reason, and be no different from birds and beasts.

"'All beings receive rewards in accordance with the good or evil of their karma. That is to say, beauty and ugliness, humble poverty and noble wealth, longevity and early death, foolishness and wisdom—things like these come about through karma. If we were born from Brahmā, everyone would be the same. For what reason would there be these differences?

"'Again, according to your laws, Īśvara created the world. His head became the heavens, his feet became the earth, his eyes became the sun and moon, his stomach became empty space, his hair became grasses and trees, his tears became rivers, his bones became mountains, and his feces and urine all became the sea. All this is something that you brahmans have wrongly propounded. The world was established through the karma of beings. How could Brahmā manage it? You [brahmans] are stupid and perversely produce deluded 403a
ideas. And yet you say you are superior. People do not accept this.

"'Again [you say that], after his life has come to an end, the brahman alone is born in heaven and others are not, for which reason [brahmans] are deemed to be superior. But according to your scriptures, those who practice good deeds are all born in heaven. If it is the case that one is born in heaven by practicing good deeds, all beings are capable of doing good and all will be born in heaven. Why is it that only other people [apart from brahmans] are inferior?

"'O great brahman, suppose someone begets four sons and gives them each a name. The first is called Happy (Nandaka), the second is called Longevous (Jīvaka), the third is called Sorrowless (Aśoka), and the fourth is called Joyous.[12] Though they were begotten by the one father and are all of the same caste, there is a distinction in the differences between the four names. The four castes of the world are also like this. Although they have the same karmic retribution, mental afflictions, and inherent desires, they have four names. Brahman, *kṣatriya, vaiśya,* and *śūdra* may not be the same in name, but there is no [distinction of] high and low in their essence.

"'Brahmans study the Vedic canon, revere and respect it, and, priding themselves on it, engender arrogance, and on account of this they deem human nature to be fixed. I shall now explain how this Vedic canon is without any truth and can easily be split apart.

"'Long ago there was a man called Brahmā, who practiced the path of meditation and possessed great knowledge and insight. He composed a Veda, which he disseminated and taught. Later on, there was a seer called Śvetaketu (White-pure), who appeared in the world and composed four Vedas. The first was *Hymns* (*Ṛgveda*), the second was *Sacrifices* (*Yajurveda*), the third was *Chants* (*Sāmaveda*), and the fourth was *Apotropes* (*Atharvaveda*). Next, there was another brahman, called Puṣya, whose group of disciples [numbered] twenty-five, and one Veda (i.e., the *Ṛgveda*) they broadly divided, making it into twenty-five divisions.[13] Next, there was another brahman, called Śuka (Parrot), who turned one Veda (i.e., the *Sāmaveda*) into eighteen divisions. Next, there was another brahman, called Good Path,[14] whose group of disciples [numbered] twenty-one, and they too turned the [*Yajur*]*veda* into twenty-one divisions. Next, there was another brahman, called Dove-seeker,[15] who turned one Veda (i.e., the *Atharvaveda*) into two divisions, and two turned into four, four turned into eight, and eight turned into ten. In this fashion, [the branches of the Vedas] evolved into one thousand two hundred and sixteen kinds in all.[16] Therefore, you should realize that the Vedic scriptures are easily changeable.

"'Great brahman, when this Vedic canon is liable to dispersion, the inherent nature of brahmans is scattered and destroyed along with [the Vedas]. Would it still exist? If it now still exists, one should not say that the inherent nature of brahmans is determined because of the Vedas. Supposing that it is scattered and destroyed along with [the Vedas], how could you say that the inherent nature of brahmans is true and unchanging? Therefore, your statement that "I alone am respectable and other people are inferior" is not so.

403b "'Again, O brahman, you pride yourself on your wisdom, are skilled in the magical arts, look down on other people, and produce the notion that you are distinguished. But now, whatever you may know, if other people study it they too can gain mastery of it. You should realize that everyone is respectable. Why are only brahmans said to be so?

"'In the past there was a seer called Vasiṣṭha,[17] whose wife was a *caṇḍāla* woman. She gave birth to two sons. The elder was called Pure (Śuddha?) and the second was called Drink (Pāna?). They both attained the path of the seer, were endowed with the five [supernatural] faculties, modified the Vedic canon, and created a method for [drawing] dwelling plans. Can you slander these two sages and say that they were not seers? Before you said that the *caṇḍāla* class is inferior and lowly. Why then are the sons of one called seers?

"'Long ago a fisherman caught a fish. When he cut the stomach open to look inside, he saw that there was a woman, jet-black in color. The seer Parāśa[ra] had intercourse with her and begat a son, Dvaipāyana,[18] who freely exercised the five [supernatural] faculties and was endowed with awesome virtues. Were the likes of these not seers?

"'A long time ago there was a *kṣatriya* called Bhīma.[19] He too attained the path of the seer. His supernatural powers were extraordinary, his wisdom was profound, he was skilled in speech, and he was quite capable of instructing brahmans. How could a person like this be lowly?

"'There was a *kṣatriya* woman called Reṇukā (Dust Mote). She had by the brahman Jamadagni a son called Rāma, who possessed great supernatural powers and was versed in scriptures and treatises.[20] In a midsummer month he was traveling together with his mother. The sun's rays burnt fiercely and the heat of the earth scorched his mother's feet, and she was unable to go on. Rāma said, "Get on my shoulders, and then let us go." At that time his mother did not accept his suggestion. They went on again for a little way, but she was still troubled by the earth's heat. Rāma made a vow, saying, "If I am truly kindhearted and gentle, filial and respectful, let the sun spontaneously disappear!" As soon as he spoke these words, the sun vanished. Later on, his mother picked some flowers, all of which were closed. His mother said to him, "Because you made the sun disappear, the flowers do not open." He promptly made another vow, saying, "If I am kindhearted and filial, may the sun reappear!" As soon as he finished saying this, the sun shone brightly.

"'These seers were not brahmans, but the magical transformations wrought by their supernatural powers cannot be circumscribed or measured. How could they be called lowly people? For this reason all castes are equal. You should marry your daughter to my son. I shall give you as much money and as many valuables as you wish.'"

Chapter III

Revealing the Truth

"Thereupon King Triśaṅku said to Puṣkarasārin, 'Good sir, listen carefully as I cut through the web of erroneous views, reveal the way to truth, and purify the path to *bodhi* for you. For making people go to heaven there are, according to your laws, five methods of sacrifice, and these sacrifices are 403c
said to be the cause of nirvana and to enable one to be born in heaven. What are the five? The first is killing a person, extracting the fat, and using it as an offering. The second is slaughtering a horse and again using the fat as an offering. The third is the extensive great offering. The fourth is the universally open offering. The fifth is the offering [made] in accordance with one's desires.[21] These are all false, and there is no truth in them. One exhausts oneself in vain and prolongs the evil destinies.

"'There are eight wholesome methods that are truly beneficial and with which one invariably gains birth in heaven and obtains good rewards. What are the eight? The first is right faith. The second is cultivating the precepts. The third is widely practicing charity. The fourth is desiring wisdom. The fifth is always respecting fellow practitioners of celibacy. The sixth is being fond of much learning. The seventh is guarding one's physical, verbal, and mental actions. The eighth is always attending closely on good friends. These eight items are methods of purification that all beings should practice. All the first seven methods one gets to hear of from good friends. Therefore, you should now contract a marriage with me and study these wondrous methods under me. You must not engender pride and forfeit this good boon.

"'Now, I shall further explain for you from beginning to end the process whereby the castes arose, and having listened to this, you must rid yourself of arrogance. When the eon first came into existence, all types of beings were able to fly, their radiance was extraordinary, their food was tasty, and their personal adornments appeared spontaneously without anyone having made them. Later on, their merit was exhausted and all [these] things disappeared.

At this time beings practiced cultivation, demarcated boundaries, and formed notions of "self" and "[other] people," or else they prided themselves on the abundance of their crops, looked down on other people, and called themselves wealthy. For this reason everyone called them the *kṣatriya* class.[22] There were also beings who did not enjoy being at home and went into the mountains and forests. They studied and practiced methods of meditation, wore tattered robes, begged for food to keep themselves alive, purified their persons and cleansed themselves, and performed sacrifices. For this reason they were all called the brahman class.[23] Those who did such things as ploughing and sowing, cultivating and planting, hunting and fishing were called *vaiśya*s. Those who robbed, traded, and had no thoughts of pity or tolerance were called *śūdra*s. Once there was also a person who was traveling along the road when his carriage broke down, whereupon he repaired it, and so he was called a *mātaṅga.*[24] Those who only did farming were called farmers, and those who went from shop to shop were called merchants. There were hundreds and thousands of kinds of distinctions like these, but in reality there were no differences in their origins and their designations were established merely as provisional constructs out of a desire to describe how the castes were not the same.

"'As for brahmans, there are further distinctions, namely, Gautama, Calf (Vātsya), Kautsa, Kauśika, Vāsiṣṭha, Kāśyapa, and Māṇḍavya. These seven
404a clans are again each divided, all producing ten groups. The eighth is called Smoky (Dhūmra).[25] There are no further different clans. You brahmans, though your name is uniform, have subdivisions. Beings at the start of the eon were also like this. At root there are no differences, but when differentiated they turn into many clans.

"'Therefore, you should now observe [the matter] carefully for the sake of Dharmic benefit and in order to cut off the false and seek the truth. You should marry your daughter to my son. Whatever you desire to ask for, I shall without fail fulfill your wish. We should hold the wedding quickly without delay!'"

Chapter IV

Questions

"Thereupon Puṣkarasārin, having heard these words, engendered great joy and experienced something unprecedented, and he said to Triśaṅku, 'Excellent! Good sir, what you say is true. In former times, what were you that you are so able in wisdom and speech? What conduct did you practice and what merit did you perform? Pray but tell me in full detail!'

"Triśaṅku said, 'I recall that in the past I was once King Brahmā, and Śakra as well, and again I was once the seer Śvetaketu (Pure Cover) and a brahman, turning one Veda into four parts. For hundreds of thousands of eons I was a wheel-turning sage-king (*cakravartin*). Wherever I was born was distinguished and wealthy, and there and then I cultivated compassion, meditation, and wisdom, extensively converted beings, and performed buddha deeds.'

"Puṣkarasārin said, 'Good sir, have you read the Sāvitra divine spell?'[26]

"He replied, 'I have read it. Listen carefully now as I explain in full everything about this spell. In the far distant past, *asaṃkhyeya* eons ago, I was a seer called Vasu, endowed with the five [supernatural] faculties, completely free and unimpeded, duly practicing meditation, and of surpassing wisdom. At the time, there was a *nāga* king called Takṣaka who had a daughter by the name of Kapilā (Yellow Head), of beautiful countenance and figure and endowed with regular features. On seeing her, I engendered thoughts of love and attachment, and on account of having produced these thoughts I lost my supernatural faculties and meditation techniques. Deeply repentant and self-reproachful, I uttered this spell. This spell has in all three sections and twenty-one syllables. Again, it has three sections, [each] with only eight syllables. Listen carefully now as I enunciate it:

> *tad yathā, oṃ bhūr bhuvaḥ svaḥ, tat savitur vareṇyaṃ bhargo devasya dhīmahi, dhiyo yo naḥ pracodayāt.*

([The spell is] like this: *Oṃ,* earth, air, sky. May we attain that excellent glory of the god Savitṛ: so may he stimulate our prayers.)

"'This is called the spell for brahmans.

oṃ jaṭilas tāpaso bhūtvā gahanaṃ vanam āśritaḥ,
gambhīrāvabhāse tatra hy ātmārāmas taporataḥ.[27]
devasya śreṣṭhakaṃ bhojanam upanām[*ya*] *pradāsyāmaḥ.*
(*Oṃ.* [The first-born, the lord of creatures,] having become an ascetic with matted hair, took refuge in a dense forest, for in that deep splendor, delighting in the Self, he rejoiced in austerities. Having brought the god's
404b best food, we shall offer it.)

"'This is called the divine spell for *kṣatriya*s.

oṃ citraṃ hi te vaiśyakanyā, atha sā kanyā arthataḥ pravīṇā.
(*Oṃ.* In different ways for you, the *vaiśya* maiden, and that maiden is indeed clever.)

"'This is called the divine spell for *vaiśya*s.

oṃ atapaḥ pratapaḥ, jīved athaṃ varṣaśataṃ, paśyed athaṃ cira[*m*].
(*Oṃ,* neglectful of austerities, practicing austerities. May he live a hundred years! May he see for a long time!)[28]

"'This is called the divine spell for *śūdra*s.

Oṃ. Wherever there is form, there is invariably desire;
Wherever there is desire, there is invariably suffering.
If one can free oneself from this desire,
One will certainly gain [birth in] the abode of Brahmā.

"'This is called the Sāvi[t]ra spell for the heavenly king Great Brahmā.'
"Puṣkarasārin said, 'What is your clan?'
"He said, 'My clan is Ātreya (Three Nothings).'[29]
"Again he asked, 'Good sir, from where do you originally come?'
"He replied, 'I was originally born from water.'
"'Who was your teacher?'
"He replied, 'My teacher was called Kāleya.'[30]
"'In your lineage group, who are the most valiant?'

"He replied, 'In my lineage there are altogether three deemed to be the most courageous. One is called Vātsya (Single), the second is called Kautsya (Oftentimes), and the third is called Bharadvāja.'

"'Who is your co-teacher?'

"He replied, 'The chanter.'

"Again he asked, 'How many varieties of chanters are there?'

"He replied, 'There are six kinds.'

"'From which clan is your mother?'

"He replied, 'My mother's clan is Pārāśa[rīya]. Such, good sir, is my virtuous conduct. This being the case, I therefore said earlier that the high or low status of all beings is indeterminate. Someone who, though respectable, commits evil is still called lowly; if a lowly person is able to perform good deeds, he is then called distinguished. Therefore, all designations of respectability are due to the cultivation of good deeds, and one is not called a superior person because of one's caste. Knowing this, you should rid yourself of pride.'"

Chapter V

Explaining the Star Charts

"Thereupon Puṣkarasārin asked Triśaṅku, 'Do you, good sir, know anything about astrology?'

"Triśaṅku said, 'O great brahman, I have mastered secrets beyond this, so how could I not know anything about a minor matter like that? You should listen carefully as I now explain.

"'Although there are many constellations, there are only twenty-eight important ones.[31] The first is called the lunar mansion Pleiades (Kṛttikā); the second is called Net (Rohiṇī); the third is called Turtle (Mṛgaśiras); the fourth is called Orion (Ārdrā); the fifth is called Well (Punarvasu); the sixth is called Ghost (Puṣya); the seventh is called Willow (Aśleṣā); the eighth is called 404c
[Seven] Stars (Maghā); the ninth is called Drawn Bow (Pūrvaphalgunī); the tenth is called Wing (Uttaraphalgunī); the eleventh is called Cross Board [of a Carriage] (Hastā); the twelfth is called Horn (Citrā); the thirteenth is called Neck (Svātī); the fourteenth is called Base (Viśākhā); the fifteenth is called Room (Anurādhā); the sixteenth is called Heart (Jyeṣṭhā); the seventeenth is called Tail (Mūlā); the eighteenth is called Winnowing Basket (Pūrvāṣāḍhā); the nineteenth is called Dipper (Uttarāṣāḍhā); the twentieth is called Ox (Abhijit); the twenty-first is called Woman (Śravaṇā); the twenty-second is called Void (Dhaniṣṭhā); the twenty-third is called Rooftop (Śatabhiṣaj); the twenty-fourth is called House (Pūrvabhādrapada); the twenty-fifth is called Wall (Uttarabhādrapada); the twenty-sixth is called Astride (Revatī); the twenty-seventh is called Mound (Aśvinī); and the twenty-eighth is called Stomach (Bharaṇī). These are called the twenty-eight lunar mansions.'

"Puṣkarasārin said, 'How many stars do these lunar mansions have? What are they like in appearance? Again, for how long are they together with the moon? What does one use for making sacrifices to them? Which deities preside over them? What lineage do they have? Good sir, pray but explain it further.'[32]

"Triśaṅku said, 'If you wish to hear, listen carefully as I explain. The Pleiades have six stars; in shape they are like scattered flowers; they move together with the moon for twelve hours; for sacrifices use curds; the fire god [Agni] presides over them, and the clan is Vaiśyāyan[a]. Net has five stars; in shape it is like flying geese; it moves together with the moon for one and a half days; make sacrifices with deer meat; it is subject to King Brahmā, and the clan is Bhāradvā[ja]. Turtle has three stars; in shape it is like a deer's head; it is together with the moon throughout one day; use fruit to make sacrifices; it is subject to the moon god [Soma], and the clan is the Deer family (Mṛgāyaṇa). Orion has one star; it follows the moon for one day; make sacrifices with ghee; it is related to the sun god [Sūrya], and the clan is the Settled family. Well has two stars; in shape it is like a person's step; it is together with the moon for only one day; for sacrifices be sure to use honey; it is subject to Jupiter, and the clan is again the Settled family.[33] Ghost has three stars; in shape it is like a painted jar; it travels together with the moon for one day; for sacrifices use peach flowers; it is subject to Jupiter, and the clan is Aupa[ma]nya[va]. The lunar mansion Willow has one star; it is together with the moon for half a day without either abandoning the other; for making sacrifices to it use milk; it belongs to the dragon god [Sarpa], and therefore the clan is the Dragon family. There are these seven lunar mansions in the eastern quarter.

"'As for the Seven Stars, five are visible and two stars are hidden; in shape they are like the bend in a river; they follow the moon for one day; make sacrifices to them with sesamum; they are subject to the god of ghosts [Pitṛ], and the clan is Piṅgal[āyan]a. The lunar mansion Drawn Bow has two stars; it is also like a person's step; it moves together with the moon throughout one day; use fruit for sacrifices; the clan is the Good family, and it is subject to the good god [Bhava]. Wing has two stars; in shape it is like a person's step; it moves with the moon for one and a half days; make sacrifices to it with shark; it is subject to the god Bhaga, and the clan is Kauśika. The lunar mansion Cross Board has five stars; in shape it is like a human hand; it moves together with the moon for one day and one night; make sacrifices to it with panic grass; the clan is Śyāmāyan[a], and it is subject to the god Tvaṣṭṛ. Horn has one star; it follows the moon for one day; make sacrifices with flowers;
405a it is subject to the god Tvaṣṭṛ, and the clan is Cait[r]āyaṇ[a]. The lunar mansion

Neck has one star; make sacrifices to it with parched barley mixed with ghee; it follows the moon for one day; it is subject to the god Tvaṣṭṛ, and the clan is called the Red family. The lunar mansion Base has two stars; in shape it is like a ram's horn; it moves together with the moon for one and a half days; use flowers for sacrifices; it is subject to the fire god [Agni], and the clan is Saṃcayan[a]. There are these seven lunar mansions in the southern quarter.

"'The lunar mansion Room has four stars; in shape it is similar to a string of pearls; it is together with the moon for one day and one night; make sacrifices with wine and meat; it is related to the loving god [Mitra], and the clan is Ālambā[yana]. The lunar mansion Heart has three stars; its shape is like a bird; it follows the moon for one day; make sacrifices to it with nonglutinous rice; it is subject to the god of heaven and earth [Indra], and the clan is Kātyāyan[a]. Tail has seven stars; its shape is like a scorpion; it is together with the moon for one day and one night; make sacrifices to it with fruit; it is subject to the god Śada, and the clan is Kātyāyan[a]. The lunar mansion Winnowing Basket has four stars; in shape it is like a cow's step; it is together with the moon for one day and one night; use the fruit of the *nyagrodha* (banyan) to make sacrifices; it is subject to the water god [Toya], and the clan is Kātyāyan[a]. Dipper has four stars; in shape it is like an elephant's step; it accompanies the moon for one and a half days; make sacrifices to it with peach flowers; it is subject to the Ferocious God, and the clan is Kālāyan[a]. The lunar mansion Ox has three stars; in shape it is like the head of a cow; it accompanies the moon for one hour; it is not necessary to make sacrifices; it is subject to Brahmā, and the clan is the Brahman family. Woman has three stars; in shape it is like barley; it moves together with the moon for one day and one night; make sacrifices with bird meat; it is subject to the god Viṣṇu, and the clan is Kātyāyan[a]. There are these seven lunar mansions in the western quarter.

"'Void has four stars; in shape it is like a flying bird; it is together with the moon for one day and one night; make sacrifices with bean gruel; it is subject to the god Vasu, and the clan is Kauṇḍiny[āyan]a. The lunar mansion Rooftop has one star; it follows the moon for one day; make sacrifices with nonglutinous rice; it is subject to the water god [Varuṇa], and the clan is Tāṇḍyāyan[a]. House has two stars; in shape it is like a person's step; it moves together with the moon for one day and one night; make sacrifices with blood and meat; this lunar mansion is subject to the god [Ahir]budhnya, and the clan is Jā[tū]karṇya. The lunar mansion Wall has two stars; in shape it is like a person's step; it goes after the moon for one day and one night; make sacrifices to it with meat; it is subject to the good god [Bhava], and the clan is D[r]āhyāyaṇ[a]. Astride has one large star, and the remaining small ones are its aides; in shape it is like half a jade badge; it moves with the moon for one day and one night; make sacrifices with boiled rice with curds; it is subject to the god Pūṣa[n], and the clan is the Eight Beauties family (Aṣṭa-bhaginīya). The lunar mansion Mound has two stars; in shape it is like the head of a horse; it moves together with the moon for one day and one night; make sacrifices with milk gruel. Stomach has three stars; in shape it is like the legs of a tripod; it is together with the moon for one day and one night; make sacrifices with sesamum; it is subject to the god Yama, and its clan is Bhārga[va]. There are these seven lunar mansions in the northern quarter.

405b "'O great brahman, I have explained in full the twenty-eight lunar mansions. Now, among these lunar mansions the following six move together with the moon for two days and one night, namely, Net, Well, Base, Wing, Dipper, and Wall. As well, there are five lunar mansions that are together with the moon for only one day: (1) Orion, (2) Willow, (3) Winnowing Basket, (4) Heart, and the fifth is called Rooftop. There is only the lunar mansion Ox that follows the moon for half a day. The rest all move with the moon for one day and one night.[34] The seven lunar mansions of the eastern quarter start from the Pleiades, the seven lunar mansions of the southern quarter start from the Seven Stars, the seven lunar mansions of the western quarter start from Room, and the seven lunar mansions of the northern quarter start from Void.

"'In addition, among these lunar mansions, seven lunar mansions are supreme: Drawn Bow, House, Base, Winnowing Basket, Room, Well, and Neck; three lunar mansions are fiendish: Orion, Willow, and Stomach; four lunar mansions are kindly: Wing, Dipper, Wall, and Net; five lunar mansions are mild: Woman, Void, Rooftop, Heart, and the fifth is called Tail; five lunar mansions are steadfast: (1) Turtle,[35] (2) Horn, the third is called the Seven Stars, the fourth is Willow, and the fifth is called Ox; and four lunar mansions are swift: Pleiades, Turtle, Mound, and Ghost. Furthermore, there are three ways in which these lunar mansions may be in conjunction with the moon:

(1) they may be in front of the moon, (2) they may be behind the moon, or (3) they may be alongside the moon.

"'Now I shall further explain for you the seven luminaries: the sun, the moon, Mars, Jupiter, Saturn, Venus, and Mercury. These are called the seven [luminaries]. With Rāhu and Ketu (Comet) they make altogether nine [planets]. These terms and matters concerning astrology and so on you should observe deeply and carefully.'"

[End of] Fascicle One of the *Mātaṅga Sutra*

Fascicle Two

Chapter VI

Observing Misfortune and Good Fortune

"Triśaṅku said, 'Listen carefully, good sir, as I further explain the good and bad omens of the passage [of the moon] through the constellations. Someone born on a day when the moon leaves the lunar mansion Pleiades[36] has great renown and is revered by others. Someone born when the moon leaves Net is distinguished and praised by all. Someone born on a day when the moon leaves Turtle takes much pleasure in angry disputation and harbors noxious thoughts. Someone delivered on a day when the moon leaves the asterism Orion overindulges in food and drink possessing fine flavors. Someone born on a day when the moon leaves Well has granaries full to overflowing and large numbers of cattle and sheep. Someone born when the moon leaves the asterism Ghost cultivates good. Someone born when the moon leaves the 405c
asterism Willow has many desires. Someone born when the moon leaves the Seven Stars is respectable. Someone born when the moon leaves the asterism Drawn Bow is short-lived. Someone born when the moon leaves the asterism Wing observes the precepts. Someone born when the moon leaves the asterism Cross Board is a robber. Someone born on a day when the moon leaves the asterism Horn is well versed in music and skilled in making necklaces. Someone born when the moon leaves the asterism Neck is good at calculations. Someone born when the moon leaves the asterism Base will become a [king's] minister. Someone born when the moon leaves the asterism Room is skilled in managing affairs and good at sales. Someone born when the moon leaves the asterism Heart is foolish and his life is short. Someone born when the moon leaves the asterism Tail has many offspring and a great reputation.

Someone born when the moon leaves the asterism Winnowing Basket is fond of meditation. Someone born when the moon leaves the asterism Dipper is wealthy. Someone born when the moon leaves the asterism Ox has renown. Someone born when the moon leaves the asterism Woman is much honored and favored [by a king]. Someone born when the moon leaves the asterism Void is bellicose. Someone born when the moon leaves the asterism Rooftop will become a commander. Someone born when the moon leaves the asterism House will become a leader of bandits. Someone born when the moon leaves the asterism Wall is very skilled at mixing perfumes. Someone born when the moon leaves the asterism Astride is very vulgar. Someone born when the moon leaves the asterism Mound is skilled in dealing in cattle and horses. Someone born when the moon leaves the asterism Stomach is very murderous. O great brahman, I have finished explaining in full the good and bad [fortune] of those born when the moon leaves an asterism.

"'Now I shall further explain the good and bad omens of towns founded when the moon leaves [each of] the asterisms. A town founded when the moon leaves the asterism Pleiades has great majesty and abundant riches, but it may be damaged by a great fire. In a town founded when the moon leaves the asterism Net, the people inside all cultivate good deeds, have abundant wealth and property, recite the scriptures, and have little greed. A town founded when the moon leaves the asterism Turtle has plentiful women and innumerable cattle and sheep, and is endowed with chaplets of fragrant flowers. A town founded when the moon leaves the asterism Orion has many delicacies and abundant riches, and the people inside are all foolish. A town founded when the moon leaves the asterism Well has great majesty and has many riches and much food and grain, but before long it will destroy itself. Though there may be wicked people in a town founded when the moon leaves the asterism Ghost, later they will most certainly become good, being benevolent and filial, cultivating compassion, and prolonging their years and becoming long-lived; there are many wind gods, and the five grains have little taste. In a town founded when the moon leaves the asterism Willow, there are many people inside who are sorrowful and resentful, like causing quarrels, and are mostly smelly and dirty. In a town founded when the moon leaves the Seven Stars, the people inside all have wisdom and much wealth and property, cultivate the precepts and practice charity, and are filial and respectful, chaste and

pure. A town founded when the moon leaves the asterism Drawn Bow has many women, is endowed with fragrant flowers and delicacies, medicinal 406a
[plants] and grains both thrive, and the people are at ease. A town founded when the moon leaves the asterism Wing has abundant riches, and the people are all foolish and browbeaten by women; the town is long-lasting and cannot be overthrown. In a town founded when the moon leaves the asterism Cross Board, the people inside are very fond of litigation, and there is an abundance of cattle and horses. In a town founded when the moon leaves the asterism Horn, the people inside are all bullied by women, and though they have riches, [the town] will be consumed by fire. A town founded when the moon leaves the asterism Neck has much wealth and property, and the people are multitudinous, avaricious, cruel, fawning and devious. A town founded when the moon leaves the asterism Base has much majesty, and the people inside are good at making sacrifices, but subsequently they will be annihilated by troops. In a town founded when the moon leaves the asterism Room, the people inside are benevolent, filial, chaste and gentle, and they respect their fathers and elder brothers, recite the scriptures, and are diligent in making sacrifices. A town founded when the moon leaves the asterism Heart is replete with riches, and all the people diligently practice the scriptural arts and are powerful and prosperous. A town founded when the moon leaves the asterism Tail has abundant riches and delicacies, and the people inside are by nature very violent; subsequently it will be damaged by [dusty] soil. A town founded when the moon leaves the asterism Winnowing Basket has many riches, and the people inside are avaricious and foolish. A town founded when the moon leaves the asterism Dipper has abundant riches, the five grains are bounteous, and the people inside are diligent in recitation and only like quarrelling.[37] A town founded when the moon leaves the asterism Woman has abundant riches, there is no millet or barley, and the people inside have few illnesses and are good at getting on with one another. In a town founded when the moon leaves the asterism Void, the people inside obey women, have many clothes, and adorn themselves with necklaces, and men and women have few desires. In a town founded when the moon leaves the asterism Rooftop, the people inside are very fawning and devious in their minds, and their greed is insatiable; later [the town] will be washed away by water. In a town founded when the moon leaves the asterism House, the people inside are all happy,

very jealous by nature, and fond of base deeds. In a town founded when the moon leaves the asterism Wall, the people inside gradually increase their profits, have abundant wealth and grain, and like giving alms. In a town founded when the moon leaves the asterism Astride, the people inside have plentiful cattle and horses, and their riches are immeasurable. In a town founded when the moon leaves the asterism Mound, the people inside are happy and free of illness, and men and women are handsome. In a town founded when the moon leaves the asterism Stomach, the people inside are
406b malodorous and unclean, take much joy in litigation, and experience sufferings. O great brahman, the founding of towns that I have just explained is all based on the good and bad [omens] of star charts. Be most sure to observe and study them. O great brahman, the founding of towns when the moon leaves [each of] the asterisms is as explained above.

"'I shall now further state the prospects for rain from the heavens when the moon is in [each of] the lunar mansions. If there is rain from the heavens in the summer months [when the moon is] in the Pleiades,[38] it will certainly be very widespread. The depth of the water on the ground will be two *chi* eight *cun,*[39] and it will mostly be continual rain that stops after ten days. If there is rain [also] in the summer months [when the moon is] in Woman and in the asterism House, autumn will invariably be very damp and the force of fires will be fierce.

"'If there is rain from the heavens in the summer months [when the moon is] in Net, there will be two *chi* one *cun* [of rain]. It will be suitable for cultivating low-lying fields, and bandits will also spring up. There will be only two illnesses, afflicting the eyes and the belly. In autumn one will obtain fruit.

"'If there is rain from the heavens in the summer months [when the moon is] in Turtle, there will be two *chi* eight *cun* [of rain]. In autumn the force of the water will be intense. There will be no invasions, roads will be clean, with nothing to fear, and people will be happy.

"'If there is rain from the heavens in the summer months [when the moon is] in Orion, there will be eight *cun* [of rain]. It will be suitable for cultivating low-lying fields. People's wealth and property should be secretly hidden away. Robbers will abound that year, and weapons should be kept at the ready. There will also be three illnesses—bodily fever, asthma, and pharyngolaryngeal pain—and many infants will die.

"'If there is rain from the heavens in the summer months [when the moon is] in Well, there will be four *chi* [of rain]. Throughout that year clouds and rain will be extremely prolific. It will rain for fourteen days without stopping in between. Warfare will break out continually, and killings will be frequent.

"'If there is rain from the heavens in the summer months [when the moon is] in Ghost, there will be one *chi* five *cun* [of rain]. It will be suitable for cultivating low-lying fields. The rain's beneficence will be timely, and in autumn crops will ripen. The noble and the lowly will quarrel with each other, birds and beasts will run riot, and there will be three illnesses: (1) boils, (2) abscesses, and (3) skin diseases.

"'If the heavens above cause rain to fall in the summer months [when the moon is] in Willow, there will be two *chi* one *cun* [of rain]. It will be suitable for cultivating low-lying fields. Adverse winds will rage, neighboring countries will bring lawsuits, and crops will ripen.

"'If rain pours down in the summer months [when the moon is] in the Seven Stars, there will be nine *cun* [of rain]. In autumn many seedlings will bear fruit. Fetuses will be injured and die prematurely, and many people will die.

"'If the heavens cause rain to fall in the summer months [when the moon is] in Drawn Bow, there will be two *chi* seven *cun* [of rain]. That year [crops] will bear fruit in autumn, but they will be eaten by others. People will have many illnesses, but fetuses will be safe.

"'If there is rain in the summer months [when the moon is] in Wing, the good and bad [omens] are as explained for Drawn Bow.

"'If there is rain from the heavens in the summer months [when the moon is] in Cross Board, there will be nine *chi* two *cun* [of rain]. That year the crops will be damaged by birds, the rain's beneficence will be minimal, and [crops] will not bear fruit in autumn.

"'If there is rain from the heavens in the summer months [when the moon is] in Horn, there will be two *chi* three *cun* [of rain]. In summer the rain is minimal, but in autumn it will become profuse. Warfare will cease after a while, and people will be happy.

"'If there is rain from the heavens in the summer months [when the moon is] in Neck, there will be two *chi* one *cun* [of rain]. Bandits will spring up, and there will be no difference between the high and the lowly.

"'If there is rain in the summer months [when the moon is] in Base, there
406c will be four *chi* [of rain]. Everything in high and low-lying [fields] will ripen. War and fire will both rage, and birds and beasts will die or be injured.

"'If there is rain in the summer months [when the moon is] in Room, there will be two *chi* [of rain]. Seedlings will ripen in autumn. People will bring disaster upon one another, and benevolence and righteousness will be completely abandoned.

"'If the heavens cause rain to fall in the summer months [when the moon is] in Heart, there will be one *chi* six *cun* [of rain]. That year there will be many illnesses, and it will not be suitable for people riding elephants and horses or for warfare.

"'If there is rain from the heavens in the summer months [when the moon is] in Tail, there will be one *chi* eight *cun* [of rain]. Grain will ripen in autumn, bandits will run wild in the four quarters, and there will arise three illnesses, (1) afflicting the eyes, (2) afflicting abscesses, and (3) afflicting ribs. Flowers and fruits will thrive, and warfare will not break out.

"'If there is rain in the summer months [when the moon is] in Winnowing Basket, there will be two *chi* [of rain]. Initially there will be a drought and later floods. In autumn [crops] will ripen. There will be two kinds of illnesses, afflicting the belly and the eyes.

"'If there is rain in the summer months [when the moon is] in Dipper, there will be seven *chi* [of rain]. It will be suitable for cultivating high fields. Waters will be very turbulent. That year medicinal [plants] and grains will all ripen. There will arise three illnesses, and they are as was explained for Ghost.

"'If there is rain in the summer months [when the moon is] in Woman, there will be three *chi* [of rain]. Water and rain will not be timely. In autumn waters will rise, and many of all those living in dependence on water will die. Warfare will be widespread.

"'If the heavens above cause rain to fall in the summer months [when the moon is] in Void, there will be one *chi* seven *cun* [of rain]. It will be suitable for cultivating low-lying fields. There will occur illnesses with abscesses, and warfare will break out everywhere.

"'If there is rain in the summer months [when the moon is] in Rooftop, there will be five *cun* [of rain]. It will be suitable for cultivating low-lying fields, and in autumn [crops] will ripen. There will be armed insurrections both within and without, and those [living] in towns will take their wives and children and flee to other regions.

"'If there is rain in the summer months [when the moon is] in House, there will be three *chi* [of rain]. First there will be a drought and later floods. Flowers and fruits will wither, and the autumn harvest will fail. Bandits will run wild, bilious illnesses will be prevalent, and many women will die.

"'If there is rain from the heavens in the summer months [when the moon is] in Wall, there will be four *chi* five *cun* [of rain]. Water and rain will overflow, and walls will collapse. There will be four kinds of illnesses: affliction of the nether regions (i.e., belly), eye ache, coughing, and bodily fever. Many infants will die. It will be suitable for cultivating high fields, and flowers and fruits will flourish.

"'If there is rain from the heavens in the summer months [when the moon is] in Astride, there will be three *chi* two *cun* [of rain]. It will be suitable for cultivating low-lying fields, autumn crops will ripen, and warfare will not break out.

"'If there is rain from the heavens in the summer months [when the moon is] in Mound, there will be one *chi* two *cun* [of rain]. It will be suitable for cultivating low-lying fields. War and banditry will both break out.

"'If there is rain in the summer months [when the moon is] in Stomach, there will be four *chi* [of rain]. It will be suitable for cultivating high fields. That year there will be a poor harvest, and warfare will certainly break out. Fathers and sons will be at loggerheads with each other, and brothers will injure one another. This is all called the good and bad of the omens of rain.'

"Then Triśaṅku said to Puṣkarasārin, 'O great brahman, now I shall further explain the auspicious and inauspicious omens of solar and lunar eclipses.[40] You should now concentrate carefully. If there is an eclipse when the moon is in the lunar mansion Pleiades, there will be many calamities in the middle kingdom[41] and disasters will invariably occur. If there is an eclipse when the moon is in the lunar mansion Net, people everywhere will encounter trouble, and catastrophes will occur frequently. If there is an eclipse [when the moon is] in Turtle, ministers will be executed. This is also the case for Orion and 407a
Well. If [there is an eclipse when the moon is] in the lunar mansion Willow, those living in mountains will all meet with disaster, and *nāga*s and snakes will without exception be exterminated. If there is an eclipse when the moon

is in the Seven Stars, people cultivating sugar cane will suffer injury. If there is an eclipse [when the moon is] in Drawn Bow, vengeful bandits will be subdued. If there is an eclipse [when the moon is] in Wing, those near reservoirs and marshes will also all go into decline. If there is an eclipse [when the moon is] in Cross Board, those who protect towns and defend them will all be destroyed. If there is an eclipse [when the moon is] in Horn, flying birds will perish. If there is an eclipse [when the moon is] in Neck, men supporting wives will also be tormented. If there is an eclipse [when the moon is] in Base, all those living near water will have disasters. If there is an eclipse when the moon is in Room, no merchants or drivers will have any profitable business. If there is an eclipse [when the moon is] in Heart, it is as was explained for Turtle. If there is an eclipse [when the moon is] in Tail, many travelers will die. If there is an eclipse [when the moon is] in Winnowing Basket, people such as those who ride elephants and horses will also fall off them. This is also the case if there is an eclipse [when the moon is] in Dipper. If there is an eclipse [when the moon is] in the asterism Ox, there will be frequent troubles for those who have left home [to become renunciants] and for those in the south. If there is an eclipse [when the moon is] in Woman, vengeful bandits will disappear and horse herders will all be brutally killed. If there is an eclipse [when the moon is] in Void, people in the north will all be destroyed. If there is an eclipse [when the moon is] in Rooftop, people who dare to perform magic and sacrifices will all be injured. If there is an eclipse [when the moon is] in House, people who make perfumes and necklaces will also all be destroyed. If there is an eclipse [when the moon is] in Wall, those acquainted with music will fall into decline. If there is an eclipse [when the moon is] in Astride, those who travel by boat will also be profitless. If there is an eclipse [when the moon is] in Mound, horse dealers will die. If there is an eclipse [when the moon is] in Stomach, farmers will be destroyed. These are called the omens of eclipses, and I have differentiated them in accordance with their essential nature.'

"Triśaṅku said, 'Good sir, you should listen as I now further explain the things that should be done when the moon is in [each of] the asterisms. When the moon is in the lunar mansion Pleiades, one should perform sacrifices, receive titular rank, repair houses, buy sundry domestic animals, domesticate cattle and horses, make vessels of metal and stone, and build hothouses [for keeping the sacrificial fire]. It is suitable for planting red flowers, constructing walls, moving house, bathing, and wearing new clean clothes. It is not suitable for weaving, litigation, or incarceration. One should repair roads, and one should make vessels of gold, silver, copper, and iron. If it rains on this day, it will certainly not be widespread. Those born on this day are very impatient by nature, intrepid, long-lived, and attentive to sacrifices.

"'A day when the moon is in Net is suitable for deeds such as ploughing, marriage, building houses, spending money, taming animals, and sewing clothes. It is not suitable for collecting debts, waging battles, or making wine. It is auspicious should it rain on this day. Those born [on this day] are compassionate and lustful, crave for tasty food, and have abundant wealth and property, and their life span is lengthy.

"'A day when the moon is in Turtle is suitable for markets, sending mes- 407b
sengers, plastering houses, planting trees, construction work, building palaces, repairing roads, wearing old clothes, and adorning oneself with necklaces, and it is suitable for sacrificing to the gods. Should there be rain on this day, it will be all-pervading. Those born [on this day] are timid, fond of sleep, lustful, clever, and wise.

"'A day when the moon is in Orion is suitable for collecting debts, repairing wells, rivers, and canals, buying cows, pressing oil, making wine, and crushing sugarcane. Cruel deeds are to be much eschewed. Should it rain on this day, the waters will invariably overflow. Those born [on this day] like hunting and are by nature fond of the taste of meat.

"'A day when the moon is in Well is suitable for making jars, taking the tonsure and receiving the precepts, and moving elsewhere to another abode. One should not prescribe medicine. It is auspicious should it rain on this day. If someone is born [on this day], he will be lustful, eat little, and like doing many things.

"'A day when the moon is in Ghost is suitable for taking wondrous medicine, wearing new clean clothes, bathing, making sacrifices, installing [someone] in the position of minister, adorning one's entire body with accessories, shaving one's hair, and construction work. Those born on this day are good to people and their life span is lengthy.

"'When the moon is in the lunar mansion Willow, [that day] is suitable for committing cruel deeds, building walls and shops, damming up water, and erecting bridges. If it rains on this day, there will be many mosquitoes and gnats, but after the rain they will abate. Those born on this day are by nature very vile, fond of sleeping, and short-lived.

"'When the moon is in the Seven Stars, [that day] is suitable for planting miscellaneous grains, erecting storehouses, becoming reconciled with foes, cultivating plants, making ploughs, and sacrificing to honored spirits. Should there be rain on this day, autumn will invariably be fruitful. If someone is born [on this day], he will be loving toward his parents, lascivious, long-lived, edacious, and invariably victorious in battle. It is not suitable for cruel deeds.

"'When the moon is in the lunar mansion Drawn Bow, [that day] is suitable for making necklaces, wearing new clean clothes, planting fruit trees, and establishing shops; it is suitable for doing good deeds, repairing houses, and employing people. Those born on this day have little hair and are handsome. Should there be rain on this day, autumn will be very fruitful.

"'A day when the moon is in Wing is auspicious for all deeds. Those born on this day are outstandingly fine-looking and clever and have a good memory. Things that have disappeared or have been lost will be recovered. Should there be rain on this day, autumn crops will ripen.

"'When the moon is in the lunar mansion Cross Board, [that day] is auspicious for everything. It is suitable for taming elephants and horses, granting official posts and making ponds; it is not advantageous for thievery. Should there be rain on this day, it will invariably overflow. Those born [on this day] are intrepid, thievish, very knowledgeable, and long-lived and have few illnesses.

"'When the moon is in the lunar mansion Horn, [that day] is suitable for sewing clothes, making necklaces, reviewing troops and deploying soldiers, inspecting storehouses, playing musical instruments, learning ship[building] and carriage[-making], making music, and doing sketches. Should there be rain on this day, it will certainly not be widespread. Those born on this day are intelligent, very knowledgeable, skilled at physiognomy, always fond of hunting, very excitable by nature, longevous, affectionate, and avaricious.

"'When the moon is in the lunar mansion Neck, [that day] is suitable for taming elephants and horses, making musical instruments, and marrying a husband or taking a wife; it is not suitable for going forth and pursuing one's
407c enemies. Should there be rain on this day, afterward it will invariably be very windy. Those born on this day are intelligent, prone to illness, and are by nature resolute and courageous.

"'A day when the moon is in Base is suitable for planting fruits, rice, and hemp, building houses, and bathing; it is not suitable for sowing beans. Should it rain on this day, afterward there will be little water. Those born on this day are handsome and very knowledgeable, have few progeny, are restive by nature, crave for tasty food, and rejoice in [associating with] good people.

"'A day when the moon is in the lunar mansion Room is suitable for spending money, and things that have disappeared are easily recovered. Those born on this day are financially very supportive of their relatives and enjoy performing meritorious deeds. Should there be rain on this day, it will invariably rise in flood.

"'When the moon is in the lunar mansion Heart, [that day] is suitable for ascending to the position of emperor, building towns, [conducting] official affairs, and engaging in commerce. Things that have disappeared are difficult to recover. Those born on this day are invariably the eldest son, very knowledgeable, long-lived, and well versed in scriptures and treatises. [It is suitable for] breaking in elephants and horses, and it is suitable for appointing officials. The wounded will die. It is not suitable for cruel deeds. It is auspicious should it rain on this day.

"'When the moon is in the lunar mansion Tail, [that day] is suitable for planting fruits and vegetables, collecting debts, making sacrifices, treating illnesses, and wearing accessories on one's person; everything else is inauspicious. It is suitable for making brewer's wort. Those born on this day have many progeny and plentiful wealth and are long-lived. Things lost are difficult to regain. It is good should it rain on this day.

"'When the moon is in the lunar mansion Winnowing Basket, [that day] is suitable for repairing rivers and canals, planting flowers and fruits, and constructing gardens; it is auspicious for people who have left home [to become renunciants], but inauspicious for everyone else. Things lost are difficult to recover. Those born on [this] day are long-lived, handsome, obedient to their parents, compassionate, and benevolent.

"'When the moon is in the lunar mansion Dipper, [that day] is not suitable for angry disputes; one does not wear new clothes, collect [debts], or make sacrifices. Those born on this day are respectful toward their parents, taciturn, and thoroughly trained in the classics. Things lost are easily regained. It is good should it rain on this day.

"'When the moon is in the lunar mansion Ox, it is as was explained for the asterism Dipper.

"'When the moon is in the lunar mansion Woman, [that day] is suitable for reciting scriptural texts, appointing ministers, making sacrifices, reviewing troops, and sending out an army. Those born on this day have few illnesses and are very knowledgeable, intelligent, and obedient to their parents. It is auspicious should it rain on this day. Things lost will all be recovered.

"'When the moon is in the lunar mansion Void, [that day] is good for all deeds. Those born on this day are wise and very learned, have abundant wealth, and are gentle and good. Things lost are difficult to regain. Should there be rain on this day, afterward there will be little water.

"'When the moon is in the lunar mansion Rooftop, [that day] is suitable for prescribing medicine, sacrificing to the gods, spending money, and [conducting] commercial transactions; it is suitable for planting hemp and barley. It is not suitable for sending messengers, installing [people] in official posts, or planting medicinal [herbs]. Things lost are easily regained. Those born on this day are by nature very impatient.

"'When the moon is in the lunar mansion House, [that day] is suitable for performing cruel deeds. Things damaged or lost are difficult to regain. Those born on this day are distinguished, amicable, and by nature quick-tempered. It is auspicious should it rain on this day.

"'When the moon is in the lunar mansion Wall, [that day] is not suitable for going to the south, and other deeds are inauspicious. Those born on this day are respectable, long-lived, and of exalted renown. Should there be rain on this day, there will be an increase of things that disappear.

"'When the moon is in the lunar mansion Astride, [that day] is suitable for disbursing gold, silver, grain, barley, and goods, erecting storehouses, and making wine; it is not suitable for building bridges, making wort, repairing
408a roads, mixing aromatics, or wearing new clean clothes. Those born on this day leave home to cultivate merit, take pity on beings, extend assistance to the poor and needy, and cooperate with their relatives. This day is good for rain. Things lost will be regained. It is suitable for building stables.[42]

"'When the moon is in the lunar mansion Mound, [that day] is suitable for building hothouses, erecting stables, breaking in chariot horses, and paying out and receiving money; it is suitable for planting grain. One should prescribe wondrous medicine and treat illnesses. Those born on this day are intelligent and handsome, will in the end win honors and favors from the king, have few illnesses, and are valiant. This day is good for rain. Things lost are easily regained.

"'When the moon is in the lunar mansion Stomach, [that day] is suitable for doing cruel deeds, determining rank, and employing people; it is not suitable for marrying a husband or taking a wife. Those born on this day forcibly take money, have much falseness and little truthfulness, and immeasurable evil, avarice, and deceit all gather in their person. Things lost are difficult to regain, and illnesses are difficult to cure. It is not suitable for going on a trip or for rainfall; it is suitable for sacrificing to the gods.

"'O great brahman, I shall now further explain the omens of earthquakes. You should listen carefully. Whenever the earth quakes, there are invariably many outbreaks of war. When one [of the four elements, namely,] earth moves, the [other] three elements (i.e., water, fire, and wind) do so too. If the earth quakes in the third month, there will be an outbreak of war before ten days pass. If the earth quakes in the fourth month, it is also as was explained above. If the earth quakes in the fifth month, there will be an outbreak of war in twenty-five days. If the earth quakes in the sixth month, there will be an outbreak of war in seventy-five days. If the earth quakes in the seventh month, there will be an outbreak of war before one hundred days pass. If the earth quakes in the eighth month, there will be an outbreak of war when sixty days have elapsed. If the earth quakes in the ninth month, there will be an outbreak of war when ninety days have elapsed. If the earth quakes in the tenth month, there will be an outbreak of war in fifty-five days. If the earth quakes in the eleventh month, there will be an outbreak of war before one hundred days have passed. If [the earth] quakes in the twelfth month, it is as was explained above. If the earth quakes in the first month, there will be an outbreak of war when ninety days have elapsed. If the earth quakes in the second month, there will be an outbreak of war when thirty days have elapsed. If the earth quakes every month throughout the year, towns in places where the earth quakes will become deserted; [the inhabitants] will flee to other countries or else resort to open spaces, and when fifteen years have elapsed they will return to their homes.

"'I shall now further explain the omens of earthquakes when the moon is in [each of] the lunar mansions. Should the earth quake when the moon is in the lunar mansion Pleiades, fires will rage and burn down towns, workers of gold and silver will all perish, and those born [at this time] will all die.

"'Should the earth quake when the moon is in the lunar mansion Net, many fetuses of pregnant women will die prematurely, fruits will shrivel up, there will be famine, epidemics and mutual killing in war, the dead will be very numerous, and the kings of various countries will also suffer decline.

"'If there is an earthquake when the moon is in the lunar mansion Turtle, medicinal trees will not thrive, and scholars secluded in the mountains and people attentive to sacrifices will all die.

"'Should there be an earthquake when the moon is in the lunar mansion Orion, grasses and trees will wither and die, rice seedlings will be damaged,
408b and travelers, petty kings, bandits, and so on will die.

"'Should there be an earthquake when the moon is in the lunar mansion Well, those living in the mountains and artisans will all fall into decline.

"'Should the earth quake when the moon is in the lunar mansion Ghost, caravan leaders, army commanders, far-traveling merchants, and kings near mountains will all perish. There will be much disastrous hail that will damage rice seedlings.

"'Should the earth quake when the moon is in the lunar mansion Willow, *nāga*s, snakes, hibernating insects, flying birds, running beasts, and those who mix together poisons will suffer injury.

"'Should there be an earthquake when the moon is in the Seven Stars, kings will have disasters, sacrifices will be discontinued, and those from distinguished clans, those of great wisdom, and those who make music will languish.

"'Should the earth quake when the moon is in the lunar mansion Drawn Bow, the four seasons will be in harmony, and those who seize men and things for tax and those who cultivate the precepts will languish.

"'Should the earth quake when the moon is in the lunar mansion Wing, merchants, those living in dependence on mountains, and grand ministers will languish.

"'Should the earth quake when the moon is in the lunar mansion Cross Board, people such as ordinary teachers, doctors, military leaders, and those good at calculations will all be destroyed.

"'Should the earth quake when the moon is in the lunar mansion Horn, it will be as was explained for Cross Board.

"'Should the earth quake when the moon is in the lunar mansion Neck, all bandits, musicians, butchers, travelers, elephants, horses, and those living in dependence on mountains will all perish.

"'Should there be an earthquake when the moon is in the lunar mansion Base, mountains will collapse, trees will fall, evil winds will blow wildly, and hail will damage crops.

"'Should the earth quake when the moon is in the lunar mansion Room, many bandits will die, flatterers will languish, and fathers and sons will be at loggerheads with each other and not obey one another.

"'Should the earth quake when the moon is in the lunar mansion Heart, great kings will have disasters, and crows, running beasts, and the valiant will languish.

"'Should the earth quake when the moon is in the lunar mansion Tail, two-legged and four-legged [creatures] and those in mountain caves will all perish. That year there will be a poor harvest, milk [of lactating creatures] will dry up, and mountains and rocks will come tumbling down.

"'Should there be an earthquake when the moon is in the lunar mansion Winnowing Basket, animals in water, those of distinguished clans and great wealth, and those possessing wisdom will all perish.

"'Should the earth quake when the moon is in the lunar mansion Dipper, those who fashion copper, iron, lead, and tin and the poor and lowly will all die, and village camps will be moved.[43]

"'Should the earth quake when the moon is in the lunar mansion Woman, kings' men, chanters, kings of small countries, and so on will all perish.

"'Should the earth quake when the moon is in the lunar mansion Void, settlements will disperse, and rich people, archers, householders, and so on will languish.

"'Should the earth quake when the moon is in the lunar mansion Rooftop, many elephants, horses, and domestic animals will die of pestilence, and carriage drivers will languish.

"'Should the earth quake when the moon is in the lunar mansion House, those who raise pigs, those who slaughter sundry creatures, those reliant on mountains and rivers, and fiendish people will languish.

"'Should the earth quake when the moon is in the lunar mansion Wall, people cultivating merit and those dependent on water will all perish.

"'Should the earth quake when the moon is in the lunar mansion Astride, there will be a great outbreak of warfare, harm will be caused to the land, and guests will become strong and hosts weak.

"'Should the earth quake when the moon is in the lunar mansion Mound,
408c brothers will kill each other, fetuses will die prematurely, three calamities will be prevalent, and great evils will gather like clouds.

"'Should the earth quake when the moon is in the lunar mansion Stomach, many bandits will die, and fruit trees will not bear fruit; the rest is as was explained before.

"'I shall now distinguish the signs of [earthquakes associated with] the three elements.[44] If, within seven days after an earthquake, there are red clouds, the sun and the moon have no light, and shooting stars fly past, this is called a quake of [the element] fire; these are not abnormal phenomena indicative of impending disaster. If, seven days after [an earthquake], there is heavy rain, it is suitable mostly for planting; that year there will be a plentiful harvest, and there will not be anything calamitous. If, within seven days after an earthquake, clouds move from east to west, their shape resembling fish and tortoises and their color jet black, covering the sun and the moon, this is called a quake of [the element] water. That year there will be much water, and it is suitable for cultivating high fields. Other unusual phenomena indicative of impending disasters are as was explained for the asterisms.[45] If, seven days after [an earthquake], a strong wind rises and the light of the sun and the moon is red, this is called a quake of [the element] wind. That year, should war break out, it will not be suitable for sending out an army, and fires will rage fiercely, burning [things] and causing damage.

"'Should the earth quake in the hour of the hare (around 6.00 A.M.), it will harm the kings of various countries and [those riding] elephants, horses, and carriages. Should [the earth] quake in the hour of the horse (around midday), it will harm grand ministers. Should [the earth] quake in the hour of the sheep (around 2.00 P.M.), it will harm sundry domestic animals and those who cultivate fields. Should [the earth] quake in the hour of the cock (around 6.00 P.M.), it will harm bandits and servants. Should [the earth] quake in the hour of the rat (around midnight), it will harm the poor and lowly as well as women. Should [the earth] quake in the first ten days of the month, it will harm merchants. Should [the earth] quake in the middle ten days [of the month], it will harm distinguished people and young children. Should the earth quake in the last ten days [of the month], things calamitous will be few.'"

Chapter VII

Clarifying Distinctions of Time

"'O great brahman, I shall now further explain the lengths of the divisions of daytime and nighttime and the seasons. You should listen carefully.

"'In winter, in the eleventh month, the day is the shortest. In dividing daytime and nighttime, there are thirty *muhūrta.*[46] [On the shortest day] daytime has twelve *muhūrta* and nighttime eighteen *muhūrta.* On the day of the summer solstice in the fifth month, daytime has eighteen *muhūrta* and nighttime twelve *muhūrta.* In the eighth month and the second month, daytime and nighttime are equal. From the fifth month the days grow shorter and the nights longer until the eleventh month, [whereafter] the nights grow shorter and the days longer until the fifth month. The lengthening and shortening of days and nights is such that they either grow longer by one *muhūrta* or grow shorter by one *muhūrta.*

"'The first day of a lunar month begins from the first day of a new moon, and the months begin from the first day of the second month.[47] The seasons begin with spring.

"'I shall further explain the divisions of the *kṣaṇa.* The time that a woman spinning yarn takes to obtain a length of one span [of yarn] is called a *kṣaṇa* of time.[48] Sixty *kṣaṇa* are called one *lava,* and thirty *lava* are called one hour (i.e., *muhūrta*). This hour is one division (i.e., *muhūrta*) of the day. In all, thirty *muhūrta* make up one day and night. These thirty *muhūrta* each have a name.

"'The *muhūrta* when the sun first rises is called "four months."[49] When the sun first rises on the first day of the second month a person's shadow is ninety-six spans long. In the second [*muhūrta*] the shadow is sixty spans 409a
long. The third is called "wealth" and the shadow is twelve spans long. The fourth is called "house" and the shadow is six spans long. The fifth is called "great wealth" and the shadow is five spans long. The sixth is called "three circles" and the shadow is four spans long. The seventh is called "face to

face" and the shadow is three spans long. The eighth is called "together" and in the middle of the day the shadow is equal to [the height of] a person. The ninth is called "foot" and the shadow is three spans long. The tenth is called "force" and the shadow is four spans long. The eleventh is called "victory" and the shadow is five spans long. The twelfth is "very firm" and the shadow is six spans long. The thirteenth is *"vasu"* and the shadow is twelve spans long. The fourteenth is "handsome" and the shadow is sixty spans long. The fifteenth is "fiendish" and the shadow is ninety-six spans long. These are the names of the fifteen *muhūrta* in a single day [during the daytime].

"'[The *muhūrta*] at sunset is called "wicked." The second [*muhūrta* at night] is called "appearance of stars." The third is called "control." The fourth is called "tranquility." The fifth is called "boundless." The sixth is called "sudden." The seventh is called *"rākṣasa."* The eighth is called "sleep." The ninth is called *"brahmā."* The tenth is called *"diti."* The eleventh is "bird's cry." The twelfth is called "ability." The thirteenth is called "fire." The fourteenth is "shadow's foot." The fifteenth is "close to a settlement." These are the names of the thirty *muhūrta* of daytime and nighttime. Thirty of these *muhūrta* are called one day and night. Thirty days and nights are called one month. Twelve of these months are called one year.

"'O great brahman, I shall now further explain the method for measuring time. The time it takes for a person to blink is called one *lava.* Four of these *lava* are called one *kāṣṭhā.* Forty *kāṣṭhā* are called one *kalā.* Thirty *kalā* are called one *nāḍikā.*[50] Two of these *nāḍikā* are called one *muhūrta.* For [measuring] one *nāḍikā,* fill [a water pot] with five pints of water and place a round tube four inches [in length, made of] gold and [weighing] six scruples, below the pot, and when the five pints of water have passed through this tube, this is called one *nāḍikā.*[51] I have finished explaining this method of [measuring] time.

"'Now I shall explain the method for [measuring] the units of distance and the *yojana.* Seven atoms (*paramāṇu*) are called one particle (*aṇu*). Seven particles are called one dust mote (*vātāyana-rajas*). Seven dust motes constitute one hare's hair (*śaśaka-rajas*). Seven hare's hairs are called one sheep's hair (*eḍaka-rajas*). Seven sheep's hairs are called one cow's hair (*go-rajas*).[52] Seven cow's hairs are called one nit (*yūkā*). Seven nits are called one louse (*likṣā*). Seven lice are called one barleycorn (*yava*). Seven barleycorns are called one fingerbreadth (*aṅguli*). Twelve fingerbreadths are called one *vitasti* (handspan). Two *vitasti* are called one cubit (*hasta*). Four cubits are called one bow (*dhanu*). One thousand bows are called one cry (*krośa*).[53] Four cries are called one *yojana.*

"'I shall now further explain the weights of the units of weight. Twelve barleycorns are called one soybean.[54] Sixteen soybeans are called [one *karṣa,* a weight of] *suvarṇa* (gold), which is twelve scruples in weight. Twenty-four scruples are called one ounce. Sixteen ounces are called one catty. Two ounces are called one *pala* (i.e., sixty-four beans). Two *pala* are called one handful. Two handfuls are called one scoop [with both hands]. Six scoops are called one *prastha.* Twenty-four *pala* are called a *magadha-prastha.* In 409b
this manner is the method for [measuring] the units of weight fully explained.

"'O great brahman, I shall now further explain the relative severity of the sick when the moon is in [each of] the lunar mansions. You should listen carefully. Should someone fall ill when the moon is in the lunar mansion Pleiades, he should make offerings of boiled rice mixed with curds to Fire (Agni), and then he will be cured in four days. Someone who falls ill when the moon is in the lunar mansion Net should make offerings of incense to Fire (Prajāpati), and he will be cured five days later. Should someone fall ill when the moon is in the lunar mansion Turtle, he should make offerings of bean gruel to the moon (Soma), and then he will be cured in eight days. Should someone fall ill when the moon is in the lunar mansion Orion, he should make offerings of milk gruel to the god of the crossroads [Rudra], and he will be cured in ten days. Someone who falls ill when the moon is in the lunar mansion Well should make offerings of fragrant flowers to the sun (Āditya), and he will be cured in eight days. Should someone fall ill when the moon is in the lunar mansion Ghost, he should make offerings of flowers to Jupiter (Bṛhaspati), and he will be cured in five days. Those who fall ill when the moon is in the lunar mansion Willow mostly die and are incurable. Someone who becomes ill when the moon is in the Seven Stars will have complications, and he should make offerings of sesamum gruel to his ancestors, whereupon he will be cured in eight days. Someone who falls ill when the moon is in the lunar mansion Drawn Bow should make offerings of fragrant flowers to the gods,[55] and then he will be cured in seven days. [Someone who falls ill] when the moon is in the lunar mansion Wing will deteriorate and be difficult to cure. Someone who falls ill when the moon is in the lunar mansion Cross Board should make offerings of fragrant flowers to the gods, and he will be cured in five days. Someone who falls ill when the moon is in the lunar mansion Horn should make offerings of bean gruel to the gods, and he will be cured in eight days. Someone who falls ill when the moon is in the lunar mansion Neck will deteriorate greatly and be difficult to treat for twenty-five days, whereupon he may be cured, and he should make offerings of flowers to the gods. Should someone become ill when the moon is in the lunar mansion Base, he will be serious[ly ill] for nineteen days, whereupon he may be cured, and he should make offerings of flowers to the gods. Someone who becomes ill when the moon is in the lunar mansion Room should for fifteen days make offerings of ghee to the gods, and then he may be cured. Should someone fall ill when the moon is in the lunar mansion Heart, he will for twelve days[56] be very serious[ly ill] and difficult to treat; he should make offerings of fragrant flowers to Śakra Devendra, and then he may be cured. Someone who falls ill when the moon is in the lunar mansion Tail should for thirty days make offerings of sesamum to the gods, and then he may be cured. When the moon is in the lunar mansion Winnowing Basket, an illness will last for eight days, and one should make offerings of sesamum gruel to the water god [Āpas]. When the moon is in the lunar mansion Dipper, an illness will last for seven days, and one should make offerings of milk gruel to the gods. When the moon is in the lunar mansion Woman, an illness will be difficult to treat for twelve days; one should make offerings of flowers to the Mountain God, and then one may be cured. When the moon is in the lunar mansion Void, for thirteen days[57] one should make offerings of ghee gruel and fragrant flowers to the gods. When the moon is in the lunar mansion Rooftop, an illness [will last] for thirteen days, and one should make offerings of ghee and milk gruel to the water god [Varuṇa]. Someone who becomes ill when the moon is in the lunar mansion House is difficult to treat. When the moon is in the lunar mansion Wall, an illness will last for seven days, and one should make offerings of flowers to the Kitchen God, whereafter one may be cured. Someone who becomes ill when the moon is in the lunar mansion Astride will invariably [be ill] for twenty-eight days, and he should make offerings of fragrant flowers to the gods. Someone who becomes ill when the moon is in the lunar mansion Mound will invariably [be ill] for

twenty-five days, and he should make offerings of barley gruel to the gods, 409c
whereafter he may be cured. Someone who becomes ill when the moon is in the lunar mansion Stomach is difficult to treat. These are called the omens of the relative severity of illnesses when the moon is in [each of] the lunar mansions.

"'O great brahman, I shall now further explain the speed with which those who have been imprisoned or arrested when the moon is in [each of] the lunar mansions will be set free. Someone imprisoned or arrested when the moon is in the lunar mansion Pleiades will invariably be freed in three days. This is also the case for the lunar mansion Net. Someone arrested [when the moon is] in the asterism Turtle will be freed after twenty-one days. [Someone arrested when the moon is] in Orion will be freed after fifteen days, in the lunar mansion Well after seven days, in the lunar mansion Ghost after three days, in Willow after thirty days, in the Seven Stars after sixteen days, in the lunar mansion Drawn Bow after ten days, in the lunar mansion Wing after seven days, in the lunar mansion Cross Board after five days, in the lunar mansion Horn after seven days, in the lunar mansion Neck after ten days, in Base after twenty-six days, in Room after nineteen days, in Heart after eighteen days, in Tail after thirty-six days, in Winnowing Basket after fourteen days, and in the lunar mansions Dipper, Ox,[58] Woman, Void, Rooftop, House, Wall, and Astride all after fourteen days. In the case of the lunar mansion Mound, it is [after] three days. It is difficult for someone arrested [when the moon is] in the lunar mansion Stomach to be freed. This is called the speed of [emancipation from] bondage and confinement when the moon is in [each of] the lunar mansions.

"'I shall now further explain the omens of moles. If a woman has a mark, purple in color, on her neck,[59] her husband will certainly be a king. If its color is black and there is a matching [mark] between her breasts, her husband will be a general. If there is a mole between her eyebrows and a matching mark on her neck, she will go through five husbands and will not want for clothing and food. If there is a mole on her cheek and a matching mark on her back, she will be a lonely widow for many years and it will be difficult for her to win a husband. If there is a mole on her ear and a matching mark on her hip, she will have a good memory and will be very knowledgeable. If there is a mole on her upper lip and a matching mark on her hand, she will be cheated by people. If there is a mole on her lower lip and a matching mark on her nether parts, she will be by nature very licentious and will not want for food and drink. If there is a mole on her chin and a matching [mark] on her nether parts, she will have naturally no lack of dainty food.

"'O great brahman, I shall now further explain the conjunction of the moon with the lunar mansions.[60] When the [full] moon is in the lunar mansion Woman in the middle ten days of the sixth month and until [the new moon] is in the Seven Stars, during that month daytime has seventeen *muhūrta* and nighttime thirteen *muhūrta.* At that time one should erect a gnomon of twelve *cun* and measure the shadow at midday—it will be five *cun* long.[61] When the [full] moon is in the lunar mansion House in the middle ten days of the seventh month and until [the new moon] is in Wing, daytime has sixteen *muhūrta* and nighttime fourteen *muhūrta,* and the shadow is eight *cun* long. When the [full] moon is in the lunar mansion Mound in the middle ten days of the eighth month and until [the new moon] is in Neck, the shadow is thirteen *cun,* and the *muhūrta* of daytime and nighttime are both fifteen *muhūrta.* When the [full] moon is in the lunar mansion Pleiades in the middle ten days of the ninth month and until [the new moon] is in Room, the shadow is fifteen *cun,* and daytime has fourteen *muhūrta* and nighttime sixteen *muhūrta.* When the [full] moon is in the lunar mansion Turtle in the middle ten days of the tenth month and until [the new moon] is in Winnowing Basket, the shadow is eighteen *cun,* and daytime has thirteen *muhūrta* and nighttime seventeen *muhūrta.* When the [full] moon is in the lunar mansion Ghost in the middle ten days of the eleventh month and until [the new moon] is in Woman, the shadow in the middle [of the day] is twenty-one *cun,* and daytime
410a has twelve *muhūrta* and nighttime eighteen *muhūrta.* When the [full] moon is in the Seven Stars in the middle ten days of the twelfth month and until [the new moon] is in Rooftop, the shadow is eighteen *cun,* and daytime has thirteen *muhūrta* and nighttime seventeen *muhūrta.* When the [full] moon is in the lunar mansion Wing in the middle ten days of the first month and until [the new moon] is in Astride, the shadow is fifteen *cun,* and daytime has fourteen *muhūrta* and nighttime sixteen *muhūrta.* When the [full] moon is in the lunar mansion Horn in the middle ten days of the second month and until [the new moon] is in Stomach, the shadow is thirteen *cun,* and daytime and nighttime have fifteen [*muhūrta*], making thirty *muhūrta.* When the [full]

moon is in the lunar mansion Base in the middle ten days of the third month and until [the new moon] is in Net, the shadow in the middle [of the day] is ten *cun,* and daytime has sixteen *muhūrta* and nighttime fourteen *muhūrta.* When the [full] moon is in the lunar mansion Heart in the middle ten days of the fourth month and until [the new moon] is in Orion, the shadow in the middle [of the day] is seven *cun,* and daytime has seventeen *muhūrta* and nighttime thirteen *muhūrta.* When the [full] moon is in the lunar mansion Winnowing Basket in the middle ten days of the fifth month and until [the new moon] is in Ghost, the shadow in the middle [of the day] is four *cun,* and daytime has eighteen *muhūrta* and nighttime twelve *muhūrta.* This is called the method of the moon's conjunction with the lunar mansions.

"'I shall now further explain the essentials of intercalation. In nineteen years there are in all seven intercalations; there is a second intercalation every five years.[62] From the fifth month through to the tenth month the sun always moves south, and nighttime increases by one *muhūrta* and daytime decreases by one *muhūrta.* From the eleventh month through to the fourth month it always moves north, and daytime grows by one *muhūrta* and nighttime decreases by one *muhūrta.* The waxing and waning of the shape of the moon are due to the distance or proximity of the sun.

"'The sun, moon, Mars, Mercury, Jupiter, Venus, and Saturn are the seven luminaries. Jupiter makes one orbit around the heavens only after twelve years; Saturn makes one orbit around the heavens in twenty-eight years; Venus makes one orbit around the heavens only after one and a half years; Mars makes one orbit around the heavens only after two years; and Mercury makes one orbit around the heavens in one year. In all, a year has three hundred and sixty-five days, in which the sun makes one orbit around the heavens; the moon makes one orbit around the heavens in thirty days. This is the method for reckoning the seven luminaries' orbits of the heavens.

"'I shall now further explain those who are governed by the twenty-eight lunar mansions. The Pleiades govern emperors. Net governs all under heaven. Turtle governs open land and grand ministers. This is also the case with Orion and Well.[63] Willow governs *nāga*s, snakes, and those living in dependence on mountains. The Seven Stars govern those who cultivate sugarcane. Drawn Bow governs bandits. Wing governs the sedentary. The asterism Cross Board governs laymen inside city walls. Horn governs flying birds. Neck governs those who leave home [to become renunciants] and cultivate merit. Base governs water people as well as insects and animals. Room governs merchants and drivers. Those governed by the asterism Heart are as was explained for the Pleiades and Turtle. Tail governs travelers. Winnowing Basket governs riders. Dipper is as was explained above [for Winnowing Basket]. Ox governs those in the south and the red-robed. [Woman governs] bandits and jesters. Void governs the middling. Rooftop governs doctors and shamans. [House governs] those who mix together unguents. The asterism Wall only governs those able to make music. Astride governs those who travel by boat. Mound presides over horse dealers. Stomach governs cultivators. In this manner one distinguishes those affiliated to the constellations.'

410b "Thereupon Puṣkarasārin, having listened to this speech, praised the Mātaṅga: 'Good sir, good sir! What you say is true. I shall now marry my daughter to your son. There is no need for any money or goods [as a bride price]. The marriage may be performed.'

"When the brahmans heard these words, they all grew angry and spoke these words: 'Why do you give your daughter to this lowly fellow?'

"Thereupon Puṣkarasārin addressed his disciples, saying, 'The Dharma is characterized by nonduality, and all are equal. You must not now engender thoughts of arrogance.'

"He said to Triśaṅku, 'You may accept the water [of the marriage rite]. I shall give you my daughter.'

"Then the Mātaṅga, having concluded the marriage, joyfully departed.

"O monks, the Mātaṅga at the time was myself, Puṣkarasārin was Śāriputra, Śārdūlakarṇa was Ānanda, and the daughter at that time was the present nun Prakṛti. Because in days of yore they were once man and wife, her thoughts of love [for Ānanda] had not yet come to an end, and so now [in this life] she followed after him."

When [the Buddha] taught this sutra, sixty monks distanced themselves from impurity, rid themselves of defilement, and attained [the state of] an arhat, and the brahmans attained the purity of the Dharma eye. When the Buddha had finished teaching this sutra, King Prasenajit and the four groups [of practitioners] joyfully put it into practice.

[End of] Fascicle Two of the *Mātaṅga Sutra*

Notes

[1] In the Sanskrit text the woman's name is given as Prakṛti, which appears in the Chinese translation of this chapter only in the chapter title.

[2] The Chinese text has *samane* for *sumane* and *samadhivardhāyija* (?) for *samabhivardhāyitum.* Otherwise the spell given here follows the Chinese transcription, which differs slightly from the Sanskrit text.

[3] The meaning of this spell may be rendered literally as "constancy, non-lapsing, impropriety." The editor of the Sanskrit text has emended *anīti* in the Sanskrit manuscripts to *sunīti* ("good conduct").

[4] *Ṣaḍakṣarī-vidyā* ("six-syllable spell"). While this usually refers to the well-known mantra *oṃ maṇi padme hūṃ,* it is also the name of a longer formula, of which several versions are found in the Chinese canon; one of these is given below, but it is not clear why it is described as a "six-phrase" spell.

[5] The Chinese transcription of this spell differs somewhat from the Sanskrit text, and the reconstruction given here is purely tentative. No translation has been given since it would be largely conjectural, but the Sanskrit version (as established by the editor of the Sanskrit text) may be quoted for the sake of comparison:

aṇḍare pāṇḍare kāraṇḍe keyūre 'rcihaste kharagrīve bandhumati vīramati dharavidha cilimile viloḍaya viṣāṇi loke, viṣa cala cala, golamati gaṇḍavile cilimile sātinimne yathāsaṃvibhaktagolamati gaṇḍavilāyai svāhā.

[6] Though the Chinese translation has "Lion's Ear" for Śārdūlakarṇa, it could be more appropriately rendered as "Tiger's Ear," as it is in the other Chinese translation. A tiger was believed to be able to differentiate various sounds with its ears, and so the word *śārdūlakarṇa* was also used to describe a wise person.

[7] The text has *dayu* ("Great Giver"), but this should probably be emended to the variant reading *huoyu.*

[8] Sanskrit *nikūjita,* from *ni√kūj,* "to warble" or "to moan, groan." The Chinese translators appear to have taken it in the latter sense, but it should presumably be taken in the former meaning.

[9] Nandana is the name of the divine garden in Indra's realm.

[10] Carrying a club shaped like a bedpost and wearing rags is one of the penances described in the *Laws of Manu* for someone who has violated his teacher's marriage bed, while

carrying the skull of a corpse as a sign of one's crime is one of the penances for a murderer.

11 This view of the origins of the four castes goes back to the "Hymn of Man" ("Puruṣa-sūkta") in the *Ṛgveda* (10.90), according to which Puruṣa, the primeval male, was dismembered in a Vedic sacrifice, with his mouth becoming the brahman, his arms the *kṣatriya,* his thighs the *vaiśya,* and his feet the *śūdra.*

12 In the Sanskrit text the fourth son is called Śatāyus, "Centenarian."

13 Here and below "division" (*fen*) presumably means "branch" or "school" (cf. Skt. *śākhā*).

14 "Good Path" is possibly a translation of *adhvaryu,* a type of priest who recited the hymns of the *Yajurveda,* based on a mistaken association with *adhvan,* "road."

15 It is unclear how "Dove-seeker" might be connected with the probable Sanskrit equivalent Kratu.

16 While the total of the number of branches or schools of each of the Vedas given in the Chinese text does not amount to one thousand two hundred and sixteen, this figure coincides with the total number of branches of all four Vedas given in the Sanskrit text, made up of twenty-five for the *Ṛgveda,* one thousand and eighty for the *Sāmaveda,* one hundred and one for the *Yajurveda,* and ten for the *Atharvaveda.* Traditionally there are said to have been one thousand one hundred and thirty-one branches of the Vedas: twenty-one for the *Ṛgveda,* one thousand for the *Sāmaveda,* one hundred and one for the *Yajurveda,* and nine for the *Atharvaveda.*

17 Vasiṣṭha is one of the seven Vedic sages; his wife was called Arundhatī.

18 Dvaipāyana is a name of Vyāsa, said to have compiled the *Mahābhārata.* Also known as Kṛṣṇa Dvaipāyana because of his dark (*kṛṣṇa*) complexion. His mother, Satyavatī, was the daughter of a fisherman.

19 The second of the five Pāṇḍava brothers (whose struggles with the Kauravas for supremacy over the land of Kurukṣetra constitute the central theme of the great Hindu epic, the *Mahābhārata*). It is possible that Bhīṣma, rather than Bhīma, is meant here; Bhīṣma, one of the main characters in the *Mahābhārata,* was known for his wisdom, bravery, and loyalty.

20 The son of Jamadagni and Reṇukā is usually known as Paraśurāma, "Rāma-with-the-Axe," and is regarded as the sixth *avatāra,* or incarnation, of Viṣṇu; he is to be distinguished from the hero of the *Rāmāyaṇa,* who is regarded as Viṣṇu's seventh *avatāra.* The following story of Paraśurāma and his mother is not found in the Sanskrit text nor, it would seem, elsewhere in Sanskrit literature.

21 The Sanskrit equivalents of the third and fourth sacrifices are *śāmyaprāśa* ("wedge-throw") and *nirargaḍa* ("unimpeded"), which are frequently mentioned in lists of brahmanical sacrifices.

[22] This explanation suggests an etymological link between *kṣatriya* and *kṣetra* ("field"), whereas *kṣatriya* derives from *kṣatra* ("dominion, power").

[23] The Sanskrit text derives *brāhmaṇa* (brahman) from *bahirmanaska,* "outward-minded," because his mind (*manas*) was turned outside (*bahir*) society, which he had left behind.

[24] The Sanskrit text has *mātaṅgama,* which suggests that the author may have understood the word *mātaṅga* to be derived from *mā tvaṃ gamaḥ,* "Don't you go [back to society]!"

[25] According to the Sanskrit text, each of the seven clans (*gotra*) is again divided into seven, and the second subdivision of the seventh Māṇḍavya clan is called Dhaumrāyaṇa, a patronymic deriving from Dhūmra ("Smoky"). The clan names given here correspond to the patronymics of seven legendary seers from which these clans are said to have been descended. Various enumerations of the founders of the seven primeval clans are found in religious literature.

[26] A reference to the *Sāvitrī,* a verse addressed to Savitṛ, god of the rising and setting sun. It is in the *gāyatrī* meter of twenty-four syllables, consisting of three octosyllabic lines, and the verse (the first of those given below in the text) is taken from *Ṛgveda* 3.62.10. It is often prefixed (as in the present instance) by *oṃ bhūr bhuvaḥ svaḥ,* a formula taken from the *Yajurveda.* Also known as the *Gāyatrī,* this is one of the most sacred verses in Hinduism. The present text gives a different *Sāvitrī* for each of the four castes, but the sources of the second through fourth are unclear (although alternative versions of the *Sāvitrī* are known for *kṣatriyas* and *vaiśyas*).

[27] The reconstruction of the Chinese transcription of this line is uncertain (*gambhīra tatra hi* [*tatrāpi*?] *rata. . .*), and the Sanskrit version as established by the editor of the Sanskrit text has been given instead.

[28] The reconstruction *athaṃ* is uncertain and the meaning unclear. The Sanskrit manuscripts have *ahaṃ* ("I"), which is, however, at variance with the third-person singular endings of the verbs *jīved* and *paśyed.* This version of the *Sāvitrī* may possibly hark back to *Ṛgveda* 7.66.16.

[29] The Chinese translation "Three Nothings" suggests that Ātreya may have been interpreted as deriving from *a-traya* ("not-three").

[30] Kāleya is, strictly speaking, the name of a school rather than the name of an individual.

[31] The Chinese text gives the Chinese equivalents of the twenty-eight lunar mansions rather than Chinese translations of their Sanskrit names, and the English translations represent the probable meanings of the Chinese names (with the corresponding Sanskrit names added in parentheses).

[32] The second question about the appearance of each lunar mansion concerns the shape suggested by the stars making up the corresponding asterism. The third question

about how long the lunar mansions are together with the moon concerns the length of time the moon takes to travel across each lunar mansion, and this reflects the spatial extent of each lunar mansion and is not uniform (see also note 34). The sixth question about lineages or clans (*gotra*) concerns the lineage associated with each lunar mansion, possibly those lineages or schools specializing in the study of each lunar mansion.

33 The Sanskrit text has Vāśiṣṭha (for Vāsiṣṭha), which the Chinese translators appear to have associated with √*vas,* "to dwell, live." In the Sanskrit text, the clan of the preceding lunar mansion, which in the Chinese text is also "Settled," is given as Hāritāyanīya.

34 This summary of the spatial extent of the lunar mansions in terms of the length of time spent by the moon in each is at variance with the figures given in the foregoing paragraphs. A confusing aspect of the Chinese translation is the seemingly inconsistent use of the word "day" (*ri*). In this summary it must be taken in the sense of "daytime" as opposed to "nighttime," which results in a sidereal month of 27.75 days, only slightly longer than its actual length of 27.32166 days. (The figures given in the Sanskrit text result in a sidereal month of 27.7 days.) In the foregoing paragraphs, on the other hand, "day" means "daytime" only in the phrase "one day and one night"; otherwise it would appear to signify a full day and night, which results in a sidereal month of about twenty-eight days.

35 Judging from the Sanskrit text and the fact that Turtle appears twice, this is probably an error for Cross Board.

36 Though the Chinese translation here and below has "when the moon leaves the lunar mansion. . . ," the Sanskrit text would suggest that this should be understood to mean "when the moon is in the lunar mansion. . . ."

37 The passage on the asterism Ox is missing in the Chinese translation, and it is also missing in most of the subsequent sections. This would suggest that the Sanskrit text on which the Chinese translation was based may have followed the system of twenty-seven lunar mansions.

38 This could possibly also be construed as ". . . in summer when the moon is in the Pleiades," but it has been translated in light of the Sanskrit text, which has "in the Pleiades in the latter month of the summer [months]." There are six seasons in the Hindu calendar, each of two months, and the two months of summer span mid-May to mid-July, followed by the rainy season. The prospect of rainfall for the coming rainy season is determined by the asterism in which the moon is residing when the first rain of the summer falls.

39 The units *chi* and *cun* (0.1 *chi*) may for the sake of convenience be roughly equated with "foot" and "inch" respectively, although their actual length varied in different periods. In the Sanskrit text, the unit *āḍhaka* (a measure of grain) is used. In the present instance, two *chi* eight *cun* corresponds to sixty-four *āḍhaka,* but there does not seem to be any strict correlation between the capacity measure used in the Sanskrit

and the linear measure used in the Chinese. The amount of rain given for each asterism is the estimated rainfall for the entire season.

40 As might be expected, those adversely affected by eclipses are by and large those governed by the lunar mansion in which the moon resides at the time of the eclipse, in which regard reference should be made to pp. 91–92 (although the correspondences are not always evident from the Chinese translation).

41 The equivalent of "middle kingdom" in the Sanskrit text is "Kaliṅga and Magadha."

42 This last sentence is probably redundant since it is repeated in the following section on Mound.

43 The section on the lunar mansion Ox is missing in both the Sanskrit text and the Chinese translation. Cf. note 37.

44 Earthquakes were explained in various ways in ancient India, and according to one school of thought they are associated with Indra and the three elements of fire, water, and wind.

45 This is possibly an allusion to the fact that in explanations of the symptoms and effects of earthquakes Indra and the three elements are sometimes each associated with seven asterisms. In the present case, this would mean that the other effects of an earthquake associated with the element water are the same as those of earthquakes that occur when the moon is in the seven asterisms associated with the element water (even though these are not identified as such in the text).

46 The Chinese translation has simply "division" or "part" (*fen*), but the Sanskrit equivalent *muhūrta* (one thirtieth part of a day, corresponding to forty-eight minutes) has been used for the sake of clarity.

47 I.e., the year begins from the second month.

48 This differs from the explanation given in the Sanskrit text, where the time it takes a woman spinning to draw out a piece of yarn that is neither overly long nor overly short is termed a *tatkṣaṇa,* one hundred and twenty of which make up one *kṣaṇa.* In common parlance, *kṣaṇa* refers to an instantaneous point of time, i.e., "moment" or "second," and in the scheme presented in the following sentences it equates with 1.6 seconds. Here and below, "span" (Ch. *xun*) refers to the distance between the tips of the middle fingers when the arms are stretched out horizontally as far as possible; one *xun* is equated with seven or eight *chi* (see note 39).

49 In both India and China the day was traditionally reckoned to begin at dawn. The names of the thirty *muhūrta* as given in the Sanskrit text of the *Śārdūlakarṇāvadāna,* divided as in the Chinese text into two groups of fifteen, are as follows (with tentative reconstructions of alternatives suggested by the Chinese translation in parentheses): (1) *caturojas* (*caturmāsa*), (2) *śveta,* (3) *samṛddha,* (4) *śarapatha* (*śaraṇa*), (5) *atisamṛddha,* (6) *udgata* (*trimaṇḍala*), (7) *sumukha* (*sammukha*), (8) *vajraka* (*sama*?),

(9) *rohita* (*vitasti*), (10) *bala,* (11) *vijaya,* (12) *sarvarasa* (*mahāsāra*), (13) *vasu,* (14) *sundara,* (15) *parabhaya* (*dāruṇa*); (1) *raudra,* (2) *tārāvacara* (*tārāvabhāsa*), (3) *saṃyama,* (4) *sāṃpraiyaka* (*kṣema*), (5) *ananta,* (6) *gardabha* (*ākasmika*?), (7) *rākṣasa,* (8) *avayava* (*nidrā*), (9) *brahmā,* (10) *diti,* (11) *arka* (*kūjana*), (12) *vidhamana* (*guṇa*?), (13) *āgneya,* (14) *ātapāgni* (*chāyāpada*), (15) *abhijit* (*abhicita*?).

50 In the Chinese translation *nāḍikā* is translated as *ke,* which originally referred to a one-hundredth part of a day, i.e., 14.4 minutes, whereas the *nāḍikā* is equivalent to twenty-four minutes. There are discrepancies between the Sanskrit text and Chinese translation (and also the Tibetan translation and various other authorities) regarding the length of the *lava, kāṣṭhā, kalā,* and *nāḍikā.*

51 This passage appears to describe a form of outflowing water clock (or clepsydra), one of two main types of water clocks used in ancient India (the other being the floating- or sinking-bowl type).

52 The Sanskrit equivalents of "hare's hair," "sheep's hair," and "cow's hair" mean literally "hare-dust," "sheep-dust," and "cow-dust."

53 The Sanskrit *krośa* means literally "cry" or "yell," which is why it has been translated in the Chinese as "cry" or "voice" (*sheng*); as a measure of distance it originally referred to the range of the voice when calling out. One *yojana* works out to approximately 7.3 kilometers (approximately 4.54 miles).

54 The Sanskrit equivalent *māṣaka* means "bean," but it may also refer to a weight of gold.

55 Here and below, where the Chinese translation has simply "god(s)," the Sanskrit text specifies the god to whom the offerings are to be made.

56 Variants and the Sanskrit text have "thirteen days." There are further discrepancies between the Sanskrit and the Chinese translation regarding the length of an illness, but these have been noted only when the Sanskrit text is supported by variant readings in the Chinese translation.

57 Variants and the Sanskrit text have "thirteen months."

58 Variants omit "Ox," but it appears in the Sanskrit text (although the number of days is given as six).

59 Variants and the Sanskrit text have "head" for "neck."

60 The lunar month was measured in some regions of India (especially in the south) from one new moon to the next and in other regions (especially in the north) from one full moon to the next. The following section, giving the lunar mansions in which the moon resides on the days of the full moon and new moon in each month, follows the former method and appears to have been adapted by the Chinese translators, for the Sanskrit text follows the latter method.

[61] From the length of the sun's shadow as measured by a gnomon, it is possible to calculate the latitude of the point of observation, and discrepancies between the Sanskrit text and the Chinese translation regarding the length of the sun's shadow as measured by a gnomon each month are a further indication that this section is not a direct translation of the original Sanskrit but a reworking based on knowledge gained by observations made outside India in a region further to the north.

[62] The first part of this sentence describes the Chinese method of intercalation, with seven embolismic years occurring in a nineteen-year cycle (also known as the Metonic cycle). The Sanskrit text states simply that there is an extra month every third year, and if this is taken to mean every third lunar year, then it tallies with the statement in the Chinese translation that there is a second intercalation every five (solar) years.

[63] The section on Ghost has been omitted in the Chinese translation.

THE BODHICITTA ŚĀSTRA

Contents

Translator's Introduction	105
The Bodhicitta Śāstra	107
Chapter I. Introduction	109
1. Awakening	109
2. The Merits Acquired as the Result of Awakening	109
3. Practice	109
Chapter II. Vow	111
1. Definition	111
2. *Tathāgatagarbha*	111
3. Peace of Mind	111
Chapter III. Supreme Truth	113
1. Definition	113
2. Ordinary People	113
3. Non-Buddhist Religious Practitioners	113
4. Followers of the Two Vehicles	113
5. Mahayana Practitioners	114
6. Refutation of the Reality of *Dharma*s	115
7. The Emptiness of *Dharma*s	115
8. Canonical Sources	116
Chapter IV. *Samādhi*	119
1. Definition]	119
2. The Meditation on the Moon	119
3. The Five Buddhas	119
4. The Four *Pāramitā*-bodhisattvas	120
5. The Sixteen *Mahā*-bodhisattvas	120
6. The Sixteen Phases of the Moon and Their Implication in Meditation	121
7. The Meaning of the Syllable *"A"*	122

8. The Practice of Meditation on the Syllable *"A"* 122
9. The Three Mysteries and the Five Stages to Realize Buddhahood 123
Chapter V. Enlightenment 125
Notes 129

Translator's Introduction

The *Bodhicitta-śāstra* (Taishō vol. 32, no. 1665) is extant only in Chinese translation. Although tradition attributes its composition to the legendary tantric Nāgārjuna and asserts that it was translated by Amoghavajra (705–774), I believe that Amoghavajra was its actual composer. This is a Buddhist tantric text and constitutes one of the most important *śāstra*s in the formulation of the Shingon theory of human-buddha integration. The term "human-buddha integration," which first appears in this *śāstra,* called *zhi shen cheng fo* in Chinese and *sokushin jōbutsu* in Japanese, literally means "the body, just as it is, is that of the Buddha." This *śāstra* claims that human-buddha integration is possible because *bodhicitta* (the wisdom of knowing the true nature of self, i.e., that the self is a product of emptiness)[1] is shared by both sentient beings and the Buddha, who in this case is Dharmakāya Mahāvairocana, the personification of emptiness.

The term *bodhicitta,* however, is interpreted differently in the *kengyō* (exoteric) tradition, the teachings revealed by the historical Buddha, Śākyamuni, and the *mikkyō,* esoteric teachings revealed by Dharmakāya Mahāvairocana. For example, the *Huayan jing* (*Avataṃsaka-sūtra*), a *kengyō* text, conceives of *bodhicitta* as the cause (*inbun*) of enlightenment, attested to in the story of the legendary Sudhanaśreṣṭhi-dāraka going through the fifty-three stages to realize enlightenment. The *Bodhicitta-śāstra* conceives of *bodhicitta* as a property inherent in the minds of all sentient beings and verifies this supposition through bodhisattva practice—the practice to enlighten others. Nonetheless, the inherent *bodhicitta* needs to be awakened. The awakening process is described in five stages: (1) understanding *bodhicitta,* (2) cultivating that understanding, (3) realizing the union between Mahāvairocana and sentient beings, i.e., mental union, (4) realizing physical union, and (5) realizing *bodhi,* supreme enlightenment. The five stages actually refer to the meditative process to realize the cultivation of *bodhicitta.* These stages are described symbolically in terms of the sixteen waxing phases of the moon.

In examining the *Bodhicitta-śāstra,* three questions that require clarification arise: First, it was said that Dharmakāya Mahāvairocana is the personification of emptiness. What does this mean? It should be noted here that the *Bodhicitta-śāstra* is a tantric text, and expresses concepts symbolically. Mahāvairocana is conceived of as a creator in the sense that emptiness is the source of creation. Creation refers to co-arising. Hence, the term "Dharmakāya Mahāvairocana" specifically represents the personification of the *dharmadhātu,* the realm of the Dharma, which is the co-arising of emptiness. Second, what is the difference between *bodhicitta* and *tathāgatagarbha* (lit., "womb of the buddha")? Both terms mean the same insofar as they presuppose that the potential for enlightenment exists within the makeup of human consciousness. In fact, the text employs the terms *bodhicitta* and *tathāgatagarbha* interchangeably. But while the history of the development of *tathāgatagarbha* thought is clear,[2] that of *bodhicitta* thought is not. That is, when and where did the term *bodhicitta* originate? Under what historical circumstances did it evolve into Mahayana thought? And what doctrinal circumstances led to differentiating the *kengyō* and *mikkyō* interpretations of *bodhicitta*?

It is clear that Kūkai, the founder of the Japanese esoteric tradition, Shingon, derived his integration theory from this *śāstra.* Finally, does this teaching in this text represent a gradual or a sudden doctrine?[3] What characterizes this *śāstra* is the term *zhi,* rendered as *soku* (as in the Japanese term *sokushin jōbutsu*). This is a synergistic term, meaning that through insight into *bodhicitta* the practitioner realizes human-buddha integration suddenly, while the awakening and cultivation of that insight occurs more gradually.

The *Bodhicitta-śāstra*

The treatise on the awakening of supreme enlightenment (*bodhicitta*) through yogic practices, based on the *Vajraśekhara-sūtra;* also known as the essence of cultivating and upholding the meditative practices for awakening *bodhicitta,* based on the teachings of *yoga-dhāraṇī.*

Translated by the Tripiṭaka master Śramaṇa Amoghavajra, 572b
a provincial chancellor, who was the examiner of state ceremonies, endowed with the meritorious rank equal to that of the three ministers (the Prime Minister and his two officials), and was the Duke of Su with the income of a district of three thousand households, he supervised civil matters, and upon him was bestowed the purple robe; he was entitled Daguangzhi (Extensive Wisdom) of Daxingshan Monastery and was posthumously called Dajian (Great Mirror).

[Chapter I]

[Introduction]

Ācārya Daguangzhi says:

[1. Awakening]

If there is a person of superior faculties and superior knowledge, he should not seek the Dharma of non-Buddhists or of the two lesser vehicles (i.e., of the *śrāvaka*s and *pratyekabuddha*s). He should instead be magnanimous, courageous, unafflicted, cultivate the buddha vehicle, and arouse this kind of thought:

> I desire to seek the most supreme enlightenment and do not seek other attainments.

[2. The Merits Acquired as the Result of Awakening]

Because the mental state of this vow is steadfast, the palace of Māra trembles 572c
and the buddhas of the ten quarters recognize it; and, constantly abiding in the realms of gods and humans and experiencing supreme delight, the practitioner does not forget this vow but remembers it wherever he is born. He vows to perfect the bodies of *bodhicitta* through *yoga* (i.e., to realize union with bodhisattvas by meditating on the *maṇḍala*). This state of realization is called the awakening of *bodhicitta* because these deities are all the same as the body of Mahāvairocana Buddha.

[3. Practice]

One who covets fame or rank produces that kind of thought and acts so as to attain it; one who seeks wealth produces that kind of thought and acts so as to attain it; and one who wills to do good or evil entertains that kind of thought and accomplishes what he has willed. Therefore, one who seeks *bodhi* should awaken *bodhicitta* and cultivate *bodhi* practices. Having awakened [*bodhicitta*], one should then know the marks of those practices. The marks are of three kinds. Now, the buddhas and bodhisattvas—who in the past, while abiding in the causal realm of enlightenment, having aroused the thought [of *bodhicitta*]—regarded: (1) supreme truth (Skt. *paramārtha-satya*), (2) vow, and (3) *samādhi* as their guiding principles, at no time forgetting them in the course of realizing buddhahood. They realized "buddhahood in the present body" (Jp. *sokushin jōbutsu*) through the Mantra Dharma alone. This Dharma is called Samādhi Dharma (i.e., the Dharma realized in *samādhi*). It is missing in other schools and is not spoken of by them. We shall discuss first the vow, second supreme truth, and third *samādhi*.

[Chapter II]

[Vow]

[1. Definition]

First, vow: the practitioner should constantly embrace this kind of thought:

> I will bring benefit and peace to all sentient beings of the world without leaving any behind, observing them in the ten directions as if they were myself.

The term "benefit" means exhorting all sentient beings and enabling them to abide peacefully in the realm of supreme enlightenment, never trying to save them by means of the Dharma of the two vehicles.

[2. *Tathāgatagarbha*]

The mantra practitioner should know that all sentient beings are endowed with the nature of the *tathāgatagarbha* (buddha-nature) and are capable of abiding peacefully in supreme enlightenment. Therefore the mantra practitioner does not employ the Dharma of the two vehicles to cause sentient beings to be saved. Thus the *Avataṃsaka-sūtra* says, "There is not a single sentient being who is not endowed with the wisdom of the Tathāgata." But because of delusion, distortions, and attachment, sentient beings do not realize enlightenment. If they part from delusion, then knowledge of all particulars, spontaneous knowledge, and unobstructed knowledge are readily at hand.

[3. Peace of Mind]

"Peace of mind" means that because a practitioner already understands that all sentient beings will ultimately realize buddhahood, he would not dare to be arrogant. Furthermore, through the teaching of great compassion, he takes the most appropriate means to bring about the ultimate salvation of all sentient beings. He offers what is sought by them, even his own life,

unsparingly, to enable them to live in peace and to bring joy to them. Since he is already intimate with them, sentient beings will have confidence in his words. It is indeed through intimacy that guidance is possible. Even if
573a sentient beings are ignorant, they should not be coerced into salvation. A mantra practitioner should lead them by skill-in-means.

[Chapter III]

[Supreme Truth]

[1. Definition]

Second, supreme truth refers to the insight that all *dharmas* are without essence. Why do they lack an essence?

[2. Ordinary People]

Ordinary people are attached to fame, profit, and the necessities of life; they devote themselves to achieving material security and recklessly indulge in the three poisons and five desires. The mantra practitioner should truly abhor and abandon these notions and practices.

[3. Non-Buddhist Religious Practitioners]

The non-Buddhist practitioners are attached to their own lives: with the aid of drugs they attain life in the palace of the immortals. Some consider rebirth in heaven to be the ultimate. The mantra practitioner should observe the non-Buddhist's view of salvation as follows: even if karmic forces are exhausted, one cannot part from the triple world because the afflictions remain to be extinguished, the seeds of retribution from the past are not destroyed, and evil thoughts repeatedly arise. Thus non-Buddhists sink into the ocean of suffering from where it is difficult to escape. You should know that the Dharma of the non-Buddhists is like an illusion, a dream, or a flickering flame.

[4. Followers of the Two Vehicles]

Of the followers of the two vehicles, *śrāvakas* cling to the Dharma of the four truths while *pratyekabuddhas* cling to the Dharma of twelve-stage causation (*pratītyasamutpāda*). Realizing that the four elements (earth, water, fire, and wind) and the five aggregates (*skandhas*) will ultimately be destroyed, they arouse a profound distaste for them: they destroy the notion of the reality of self and cultivate the original Dharma, eventually attaining their due level of realization—arriving to great nirvana and regarding this as the ultimate destination.

The mantra practitioner should thus observe: though the followers of the two vehicles destroy the notion of the reality of self, they still cling to the notion of the reality of *dharma*s, and although they purify their minds (*manas*), they do not understand anything beyond that. Further, by realizing the fruit [of their respective paths]—the product of eons of practices—and by destroying both body and mind, they end up reaching nirvana, which is like a vast empty space, deep and tranquil. Those of determined nature (*śrāvaka*s and *pratyeka-buddha*s) find it difficult to awaken [*bodhicitta* and are] only able to give rise to it after completing the full term of *kalpa*s. Those of indeterminate nature do not speak of *kalpa* limits. Meeting the proper conditions they directly convert to the Mahayana, depart from the "city of mirage," and transcend the triple world because of their long-developed faith in the Buddha. And through the skill-in-means of buddhas and bodhisattvas and through skill-in-means, they will finally awaken the great mind. From the ten stages of faith—going through the following stages and passing through the time of three incalculable *kalpa*s of arduous practices—they will realize buddhahood. It is already clear that the wisdom of *śrāvaka*s and *pratyekabuddha*s is inferior and is not to be indulged in.

[5. Mahayana Practitioners]

Furthermore, among sentient beings, there are those who are awakened to the Mahayana and carry out bodhisattva practices, leaving no Dharma practice uncultivated. They practice through three incalculably long *kalpa*s, observing the six perfections and innumerable bodhisattva practices to the fullest extent, and then realize the buddha fruit. These are graded practices that require a considerable span of time.

The mantra practitioner, having observed the limits of the former, again gives rise to the motivation to bring benefit and comfort to all sentient beings in their worlds without leaving anyone behind. By the determination generated from his great compassion, he permanently transcends the sphere of the practices of the non-Buddhists and the followers of two vehicles. He furthermore cultivates the supreme teachings of *yoga* that enable entry into buddhahood directly from the level of an ordinary person. Thus he transcends the bodhisattva stages. He also deeply understands that all *dharmas* are without essence. Why do they lack an essence? The gist of this was explained above. 573b

[6. Refutation of the Reality of *Dharmas*]

Now, the Dharma of the lost way arises from deluded conceptualization, and continues to develop. This brings about immeasurable and limitless afflictions and transmigration through the six destinies. If one awakens, deluded conceptualizations are terminated and various *dharmas* are extinguished. Therefore they lack self-nature. Furthermore, the compassion of buddhas arises from the truth to save and embrace sentient beings. Like a physician who prescribes the most appropriate medicine for a disease, the Buddha bestows various teachings according to [various beings' capacities] and each affliction receives its own antidote. But just as someone would employ a raft to reach the other shore but would abandon it once they have reached that shore, we should likewise abandon the Dharma that enabled us to conquer delusion, because *dharmas* have no essence. As the *Mahāvairocanābhisaṃbodhi-sūtra* says, "*Dharmas* are without marks. Their marks are the marks of empty space."[4] The realization of this state of understanding is called the supreme *bodhi*.

[7. The Emptiness of *Dharmas*]

You should know that all *dharmas* are empty of an essence. Why? Having realized that *dharmas* are originally unarisen, the essence of the mind is automatically thus. Hence, not having the view of body and mind, one abides in quiescent equality, the cognition the ultimate truth, which disallows retrogression. If delusion does arise, one would recognize it but would not follow it; when delusion ceases, the mind as the source of all *dharmas* will become void. Here myriad virtues are perfected and their marvelous function is infinite. Therefore the buddhas of the ten directions consider the supreme truth and practice of the vow as their discipline. Those equipped with this state of mind are capable of turning the Dharma wheel and bringing benefits to both themselves and others.

[8. Canonical Sources]

Thus the *Avataṃsaka-sūtra* says:

Compassion is the light and wisdom is its guiding principle,
  the two merge as skill-in-means.
In the purified mind of faith-and-understanding,
  there is the immeasurable power of the Tathāgata.
Unobstructed knowledge manifests:
  This knowledge is self-realized, not acquired through the aid of others.
All complete, he is identical with the Tathāgata,
  having awakened to the supreme state.
If a child of the Buddha awakens for the first time,
  with a precious jewel-mind such as this,
He will surpass the stage of ordinary people
  and enter the level of buddha practices.
He is born in the household of the Tathāgata,
  an infallible clan.
He is equal to the buddhas,
  and, at the end, he will perfect supreme *bodhi.*
Having realized this state, even slightly,
  he enters the stage of joy, *pramuditā.*
His mind immovable,
  he is like the king of a great mountain.[4]

The *Avataṃsaka-sūtra* further says, "In each ground (*bhūmi*), from the first ground up to the tenth ground, great compassion is the base."[6]

The *Amitāyurdhyāna-sūtra* says, "Buddha-mind is the great compassion."[7]

The *Nirvāṇa-sūtra* says, "O Cunda, though your body is of mortals, your mind is the same as buddhas."[8] It further says:

573c The Medicine King, the Buddha, pities the beings of the world;
  His body and wisdom are tranquil.
Within the Dharma of no-self, he realizes the true self;
  Therefore I pay homage to the Supreme One.
Having awakened, there is no distinction
  between initial and ultimate enlightenment.

Between the two, it is initial enlightenment that is difficult.
For not yet having enlightened oneself, one is supposed to enlighten others.
Thus I pay homage to initial awakening.
If one has realized initial awakening, he is the master of gods and humans, surpassing the *śrāvaka* and *pratyekabuddha.*
This type of awakening transcends the triple world.
Therefore it is called "unsurpassed."[9]

The *Mahāvairocanābhisaṃbodhi-sūtra* says, "*Bodhicitta* is the cause, compassion its root, and skill-in-means its end result."[10]

[Chapter IV]

[*Samādhi*]

[1. Definition]

Third, *samādhi:* How should a mantra practitioner, having thus contemplated, realize supreme *bodhi*?

[2. The Meditation on the Moon]

You should know that all beings inherently dwell in the great enlightenment of Samantabhadra Bodhisattva, [who represents the attributes of *bodhicitta*]; that though they are endowed with *bodhicitta,* they are also bound by the afflictions of greed, hatred, and delusion; that through the great compassion of the buddhas—who, through their wisdom of skill-in-means, teach this profound secret *yoga*—the practitioner is able to meditate on the discs of the sun and moon within his mind.

Through this meditation, he sees his original state of mind (*bodhicitta*), which is tranquil and pure like the light of a full moon covering space without discrimination. This state of mind is called complete enlightenment (the perfection of the cognizer); it is also called pure *dharmadhātu* (the perfection of the cognized); and it is also called the sea of the perfection of the wisdom of reality (the union of the cognizer and the cognized). Its ability in *samādhi* to contain a variety of immeasurable precious jewels is like a full moon's ability to contain its pureness and brilliance.

Why? Because all beings are endowed with the mind of Samantabhadra: one sees one's own mind like the disc of the moon.

Why is the disc of the moon employed as a simile? Because a perfect full moon is like *bodhicitta.* The moon disc has sixteen phases. This is a metaphor for the sixteen bodhisattvas, from Vajrasattva to Vajrasaṃdhi, realized in *yoga.*

[3. The Five Buddhas]

Among the thirty-seven deities [of the Vajradhātu Maṇḍala], each buddha of the five quarters represents one type of cognition. The five buddhas are:

(1) Akṣobhya Buddha of the east. He is also called "indestructible cognition" (*vajra-jñāna*) because he perfects mirrorlike cognition (*ādarśa-jñāna*).

(2) Ratnasaṃbhava Buddha of the south. He is also called "investiture cognition" (*abhiṣeka-jñāna*) because he perfects the cognition of equality (*samatā-jñāna*).

(3) Amitābha Buddha of the west. He is also called "lotus cognition" (*padma-jñāna*) because he perfects the cognition that deals with discriminative observation (*pratyavekṣaṇā-jñāna*). He is also called the "cognition that turns the Dharma wheel" (*dharmacakra-pravartana-jñāna*).

(4) Amoghasiddhi Buddha of the north. He is also called the "cognition of perfecting all works" (*karma-jñāna*), i.e., the cognition to implement insight into practice (*kṛtyānuṣṭhāna-jñāna*).

(5) Mahāvairocana Buddha of the center. He is the fundamental buddha because he represents the cognition of the world of Dharma (*dharmadhātu*).

[4. The Four *Pāramitā*-bodhisattvas]

574a From the four buddha-cognitions (i.e., the first four buddha-cognitions) emanate the four perfecting [*pāramitā*-]bodhisattvas [who are offered to the fifth buddha, Mahāvairocana]. The four *pāramitā*-bodhisattvas of Mahāvairocana are: (1) Vajra[-pāramitā], (2) Ratna[-pāramitā], (3) Dharma[-pāramitā], and (4) Karma[-pāramitā].

They are the mothers who give birth to and nurture all deities of the three time periods.

[5. The Sixteen *Mahā*-bodhisattvas]

From here, the vow hand gestures (*mudrās*) are perfected and the four buddhas emanate from Dharmadhātu Mahāvairocana. Each buddha of the four quadrants embraces four bodhisattvas:

(1) Akṣobhya Buddha of the east embraces the four bodhisattvas Vajrasattva, Vajrarāja, Vajravāśin, and Vajrasādhu.

(2) Ratnasaṃbhava Buddha of the south embraces Vajraratna, Vajraprabha, Vajraketu, and Vajrahāsā.

(3) Amitābha Buddha of the west embraces Vajradharma, Vajratīkṣṇa, Vajrahetu, and Vajrabhāṣa.

(4) Amoghasiddhi Buddha of the north embraces Vajrakarma, Vajrarakṣa, Vajradaṃṣṭra, and Vajrasaṃdhi.

Each of the buddhas of the four quarters thus embraces four bodhisattvas, making a total of sixteen great [*mahā-*]bodhisattvas.

Of the thirty-seven deities, excluding the five buddhas, the four *pāramitā*-bodhisattvas [of Mahāvairocana], the four *saṃgraha*-bodhisattvas [Vajrānkuśa, Vajrapāśa, Vajrasphoṭa, and Vajrāveśa, offered to the four buddhas by Mahāvairocana,] and the eight *pūjā*-bodhisattvas [Vajradhūpā, Vajrapuṣpā, Vajrālokā, Vajragandhā, Vajralāsyā, Vajramālā, Vajragītā, and Vajranṛityā, offered to the four buddhas by Mahāvairocana]—of which the last two groups (i.e., the four *saṃgraha*-bodhisattvas and the eight *pūjā*-bodhisattvas) are a later development—we are thus talking about the sixteen bodhisattvas encompassed by the buddhas of the four quarters. So the *Mahāprajñāpāramitā-sūtra* says:

> There are sixteen meanings of emptiness—from the emptiness of the six sense organs and the six sense fields (*adhyātma-śūnyatā*) to the emptiness of self-nature and the emptiness of the emptiness of self-nature (*abhāva-svabhāva-śūnyatā*).[11]

[6. The Sixteen Phases of the Moon and Their Implication in Meditation]

There is an essence of purity, fully prepared to perform practices, in the mind of all sentient beings. This essence is extremely subtle, pure, and bright. Though it transmigrates within the six destinies (*gati*), it does not change, like the light-essence that does not change in any one of the sixteen phases of the moon. A part of the light of the moon is absorbed by the sun, such as at the time of the new moon; at that time, the nature of its light is not manifested, but afterward the moon arises, increasing its brightness day by day, until it reaches fullness after the fifteenth day.

Therefore, a meditation practitioner should first arouse the essence of brightness (*bodhicitta*), which is inherent in the mind by meditating on the syllable *"A";* and he should gradually purify and brighten it and realize the ultimate cognition of non-arising (*ādyanutpāda-jñāna*).

[7. The Meaning of the Syllable *"A"*]

The syllable *"A"* signifies that all *dharma*s are originally non-arisen. In interpreting the syllable *"A,"* the commentary on the *Mahāvairocanābhisaṃbodhi-sūtra* gives five meanings:

(1) The syllable *"A"* signifies the thought of enlightenment, *bodhicitta.*

(2) The syllable *"Ā"* signifies the practice: for realizing enlightenment, *bodhi.*

(3) The syllable *"AM"* signifies the realization of enlightenment.

(4) The syllable *"AḤ"* signifies supreme enlightenment, *parinirvāṇa.*

(5) The syllable *"ĀH"* signifies wisdom complete with skill-in-means.

Furthermore, we can match the meaning of the syllable *"A"* with the words "to reveal," "to indicate," "to realize," and "to enter"—terms found in the *Lotus Sutra.*

(1) "To reveal" means to reveal the Buddha's wisdom-based view, that is, to reveal his *bodhi* and nirvana as in the case of the syllable *"A,"* which signifies the thought of enlightenment (*bodhicitta*).

(2) "To indicate" means to indicate the Buddha's wisdom, as in the case of the syllable *"Ā,"* which signifies practice, the indicator of *bodhi.*

574b (3) "To realize" means to realize the Buddha's wisdom, as in the case of the syllable *"AṂ,"* which signifies the realization of *bodhi.*

(4) "To enter" means to enter the realm of the Buddha's wisdom, which signifies nirvana. It refers to "all-complete perfection" and corresponds to the syllable *"ĀH,"* meaning the perfection of the wholesome skill-in-means.

[8. The Practice of Meditation on the Syllable *"A"*]

The meditation on the syllable *"A"* is designed to praise the essence of that syllable—symbolizing the five inherent meanings of *bodhicitta.* This statement of praise is described in verse as follows:

The eight-petal white lotus is within easy reach;
the syllable *"A"* manifests its pure brilliance.

The *mudrā* with hands placed together incorporates both meditation and wisdom.
It invites the tranquil wisdom of the Tathāgata.[12]

One who encounters the syllable *"A"* should meditate on it with true determination and contemplate on the perfect brilliance of pure consciousness: if one sees it just for a moment, he is the one who has realized supreme truth; if one constantly sees it, he will enter the first bodhisattva stage (*bhūmi*); if this vision gradually increases, then it pervades the limits of the *dharmadhātu,* and becomes equal to space, he would be at perfect liberty, complete with knowledge of all particulars. The one who cultivates yogic contemplation should cultivate the practices of the three mysteries in all detail and realize the essence of the five stages to realize buddhahood.

[9. The Three Mysteries and the Five Stages to realize Buddhahood]

The three mysteries are:

(1) Physical action (*kāya-guhya*): performing *mudrās* to summon the hosts of deities.

(2) Vocal action (*vāg-guhya*): chanting mantras, making each word completely clear and understanding them without error.

(3) Mental action (*mano-guhya*): abiding in *yoga,* coming into union with the pure moon that has reached its fullness, and meditating on *bodhicitta.*

The five stages to realize buddhahood are:

(1) The stage of penetration, becoming aware of *bodhicitta.*

(2) The stage of cultivating *bodhicitta.*

(3) The stage of perfecting the *vajra*-mind, the realization of the union of "knower" and "known."

(4) The stage of perfecting the *vajra*-body, the realization of the physical union of a human being and the Buddha.

(5) The stage of realizing the supreme *bodhi* and the attainment of the adamantine body.

If one has completed these stages, one has perfected the body of the presiding deity.

[Chapter V]

[Enlightenment]

What is fully revealed [in one's body and mind] is the body and mind of Samantabhadra. What is fully realized is identical to what the buddhas of the ten directions have realized. Though the period of time required for practice and realization might differ throughout the ages when one awakens, there should be no concept of time: the mind of an ordinary person is like a closed lotus bud and the mind of the Buddha is like a blooming lotus bud. If this meditation is perfected, all things within the ten directions, whether pure or defiled, as well as the distinction between sentient beings of the six destinies, between the practices of the three vehicles, among the processes from creation down to destruction of the worlds of the three time periods, between various kinds of karma of sentient beings, among the marks of the causal aspect of bodhisattva practices, and among the buddhas of the three time periods—all will be revealed and one will realize the body of the Buddha and fulfill all the practices and vows of Samantabhadra. Therefore the *Mahā-vairocanābhisaṃbodhi-sūtra* says, "The true state of mind such as this is what the past buddhas have proclaimed."[12]

Question: It was said that because the adherents of the two vehicles cling 574c
to *dharma*s, they do not realize buddhahood. Now, one is encouraged to cultivate *bodhicitta* and *samādhi*. What is the difference?

Answer: Because the adherents of the two vehicles cling to the notion of the reality of *dharma*s, they will consummate this kind of meditation only after a long period; they will remain submerged in the realm of emptiness and stagnate in the realm of tranquility; they would be limited by *kalpa* requirements as a condition to enlightenment. But they would subsequently be awakened to this great state of realization riding through the gate of the practices of goodness in a distracted state (the exoteric approach), they will pass through innumerable *kalpa*s. For these reasons, these practices should be abandoned. They should not be relied upon.

Now, though the mantra practitioner already has rejected the reality of self and *dharma*s and has acquired the wisdom to correctly see reality, he is, nevertheless, incapable of realizing the Tathāgata's knowledge of all-knowledge, because of the separation from his original nature from beginningless time. He therefore seeks the profound path, practices the three mysteries in due order, and enters the buddha stage from the stage of an ordinary person. The meditation of the Mantra Dharma enables the practitioner to penetrate the true nature of the buddhas, to be aware of the true nature (*dharmakāya*) of the buddhas, to realize the wisdom of the world of *dharma*s (*dharmadhātu-svabhāva-jñāna*), and to perfect four aspects of Mahāvairocana Buddha—*dharmakāya,* the truth body; *saṃbhogakāya,* the means body; *nirmāṇakāya,* the historically transformed body; and *niṣyandakāya,* the body that enters the six destinies in order to save all beings. The practitioner who has not yet observed the meditation of the Mantra Dharma would not gain these insights. Therefore one should cultivate the understanding of the Mantra Dharma.

Hence, the *Mahāvairocanābhisaṃbodhi-sūtra* says, "Perfection originates from the mind."[14]

The *Vajraśekhara-sūtra* says:

> When Sarvārthasiddha Bodhisattva first sat in the *vajra*-seat and attained the supreme path, he was endowed with the state of the buddhas and realized its fruition.[15]

If someone at the present time, with determination, practices the teachings as prescribed by the Mantra school, the content of this meditation would be revealed to him even without his leaving his seat and he would perfect the body of the Buddha.

Therefore the *Mahāvairocana-sūtra,* in the "Chapter on the Rites of Worship" says,

> If the practitioner's strength does not increase, he should dwell in the realm of the Mantra Dharma and only meditate on *bodhicitta.*
>
> The Buddha explained that embodied in [the Mantra Dharma] are ten thousand virtues that enable the practitioner to gain insight into the Dharma of *bodhicitta.*[16]

This is because *bodhicitta* is able to contain the virtues of all buddhas. If this *bodhicitta* is realized through practice, the practitioner will then become the master of all teachings; if he returns to the realm of inherent enlightenment, he will dwell in the buddha land of mysterious adornment. Without arising from his seat, he would perfect all buddha works.

Bodhicitta is praised as follows: if a person who seeks the wisdom of the Buddha realizes *bodhicitta,* with the body born of his father and mother, he will immediately realize the state of great enlightenment (*mahābodhi*).

Notes

1 The *Mahāvairocana-sūtra,* T.1564.30:1c.

2 See Jikidō Takasaki, *Nyoraizō shisō no keisei* (Tokyo: Shunjusha, 1974).

3 The terms "gradual" and "sudden" were conceived of in fifth-century China, after Kumārajīva had translated many Mahayana sutras. The Chinese, faced with the task of sorting out the mass of texts, developed the *panjiao* system of classifying and evaluating the contents of these texts. The *panjiao* systematizers conceived of the limits of the gradual approach and the superiority of sudden approach. The gradual approach relies on reason and inference, establishes proposition, and subjects it to a philosophical critique in order to validate its truth-claim, while the sudden approach relies on intuition and direct cognition and validates its truth-claim experientially.

4 T.848.18:1c5.

5 T.279.10:184a4–13.

6 This phrase, as presented here, cannot be located in the *Huayan jing* (*Avataṃsaka-sūtra*).

7 T.365.12:343c2.

8 T.374.12:372b26–27.

9 T.374.12:590a19–24.

10 T.848.18:1b29–c1.

11 See, for example, T.220.5:13b22–29.

12 T.876.18:328b16–17.

13 T.848.18:22a17.

14 T.848.18:19b28.

15 T.865.18:207c10.

16 T.848.18:45b29–c2.

Glossary

abhiṣeka (Jp. *kanjō*): A rite of inauguration, an anointing or consecrating ritual act. In India it means the religious act of sprinkling water upon a king's head as an act of initiation.

adhiṣṭhāna (Jp. *kaji*): Empowerment or consecration. It refers to the transference of Buddha's power and the response to it by sentient beings.

afflictions (Skt. *kleśa*): Affective disorders, defilement(s), mental disturbances, emotional negativity. All of the thoughts, words, actions, and emotions that arise and cease based on nescience and desire that keep human beings trapped in the cycle of birth and death, and which result in suffering. Buddhism teaches methods for attaining nirvana/enlightenment as a means of eliminating the afflictions.

akṣara-cakra (Jp. *jirin*): The wheel (*cakra*) of the seed syllable *A*. *See also bīja.*

Amoghavajra (705–774): A prolific translator who became one of the most politically powerful Buddhist monks in Chinese history, acknowledged as one of the eight patriarchs of the doctrine in Shingon lineages. Born in Samarkand, he went to China at the age of ten after his father's death. In 719, he was ordained into the sangha by Vajrabodhi and became his disciple. After all foreign monks were expelled from China in 741, he and some associates went on a pilgrimage to gather texts, visiting Sri Lanka, Southeast Asia, and India. He returned to China in 746 with some five hundred volumes. *See also* Shingon.

arhat: A saint who has freed himself from the cycle of birth and death by completely eradicating all passions; arhatship is the highest of the four stages of spiritual attainment in the Theravāda and other mainstream schools of Buddhism.

bīja: A seed letter or syllable, such as *A, oṃ, hūṃ, aṃ, aḥ, etc.,* which symbolizes the essence of the certain nature and power of a deity, Dharma, and action. Normally seed syllables are expressed in one Sanskrit letter and reveal many meanings.

bodhi: Awakening, enlightenment.

bodhicitta: Lit., the mind (*citta*) of enlightenment or awakening (*bodhi*). The awakened mind; the aspiration to realize *bodhi*-wisdom, i.e., perfect enlightenment.

bodhisattva: A Buddhist practitioner intent on the attainment of enlightenment based on profoundly altruistic motivations (*bodhicitta*). The bodhisattva is the model practitioner in the Mahayana tradition, one who dedicates his or her efforts to the salvation of other beings. This concept is used in Mahayana texts to distinguish from the earlier Indian notion of the arhat, who also attains a form of enlightenment but whose realization is considered to be inferior due to the individual orientation of the practices pursued in its attainment. *See also* arhat; *bodhicitta;* Mahayana.

brahman (Skt. *brāhmaṇa*): A member of the priestly class, the highest of the four castes. *See also* four castes.

buddha-nature: The possession by sentient beings of the innate buddha mind, indicating the potential to actualize buddhahood. Buddha-nature is understood as being not fully actualized prior to the full attainment of buddhahood, thus sentient beings are required to purify themselves through practice to achieve its realization.

caṇḍāla: An untouchable, below the lowest of the four castes, born of a *śūdra* father and a brahman mother; also used as a generic term for any untouchable or outcaste. *See also* four castes; *śūdra.*

delusion/ignorance (Skt. *avidyā*): The fundamental misunderstanding of reality that underlies all suffering; the first of the twelve links of twelve-stage causation. Rather than a lack of factual knowledge, delusion or ignorance is a basic error in perception that prevents people from seeing things as they really are, i.e., that all things are ultimately impermanent and lack inherent self. *See also* twelve-stage causation.

determined nature: A theory of the Yogācāra school that teaches the discrimination of the innate capacities of temperaments of sentient beings into five types: (1) the nature predetermined for *śrāvaka* practices; (2) the nature predetermined for *pratyeka-buddha* practices; these first two are commonly taken together as those with "two-vehicle proclivities"; (3) the nature predetermined for bodhisattvas, whose members will ultimately attain the full enlightenment of a buddha; (4) the indeterminate nature, whose members inherently possess the potential to attain the goals of two or three of the groups above; (5) the nature lacking capacity for enlightenment (*icchantika*). *See also* bodhisattva; *pratyekabuddha; śrāvaka;* two vehicles; Yogācāra.

dhāraṇī: Verbal formulae or mystical verses to be chanted. They reveal the essence or powers of Dharma and deity in the form of praise. A *dhāraṇī* is usually a long verse, while a mantra is a shorter verse. *See also* mantra.Dharma: The Buddhist teaching or doctrine; ultimate truth or reality.

dharma-cakra: The wheel of the law, or teaching, a symbol of the Buddha's sphere of influence.

dharmadhātu: The underlying principle of reality. In Sinitic forms of Mahayana teaching, the term refers to a religious basis or principle—the origin of all things. In this kind of teaching, where the whole universe is taken as phenomena, it is understood as the manifestation of true thusness.

Dharma eye (*dharmacakṣus*): One of five types of vision; refers to the clear perception of all phenomena. *See also* five supernatural faculties.

dharmakāya ("Dharma body"): The "reality body," "truth body"; in general in the Mahayana the Dharma body is a term for absolute existence, the manifestation of all existences—the true body of reality, or Buddha as eternal principle; the body of essence that is pure, possesses no marks of distinction, and is the same as emptiness. One of the three bodies (*trikāya*) of the Buddha. *See also* Dharma; three bodies.

Esoteric tradition (Skt. Mantrayāna/Tantrayāna/Vajrayāna): A school of Buddhism, originating in India, that developed its system of philosophy borrowing from Madhyamaka and Yogācāra thought, and which had extensive influence in Tibet as well as considerable influence in China and Japan. The hallmark of Esoteric traditions is reliance on mystical formulae called mantra and *dhāraṇī*. As the school developed, texts were written that focused on esoteric practices such as these. See also *dhāraṇī;* Madhyamaka; mantra; *mikkyō;* Shingon; Yogācāra.

five aggregates (Skt. *skandha*): The five *skandha*s are the division of matter and mind into five categories—form, feeling, perception, impulse, and consciousness.

five desires: Five kinds of desire that arise from attachment to the objects of the eyes, ears, nose, tongue, and body. Also a reference to the five sense objects of form, sound, odor, taste, and tactility that are the cause of these desires.

five supernatural faculties (*pañcābhijñā*): Five supernatural powers—(1) supernatural vision, (2) supernatural hearing, (3) the ability to know others' thoughts, (4) the ability to know former lives, and (5) the ability to perform miracles such as appearing anywhere at will.

four castes: The four main classes into which Indian society was divided; also referred to as the "four classes." *See also* brahman; *kṣatriya; śūdra; vaiśya.*

four groups of practitioners (*catuṣpariṣad*): The four categories of Buddhist followers—monks, nuns, laymen, and laywomen.

gandharva: A class of heavenly beings, famed for their musical skills.

karma (Jp. *katsuma*): Lit., "action"; in the Shingon tradition, the term "karma" means more than its literal meaning, referring to the dynamic, creative action toward enlightenment. More precisely, it denotes a cosmological act of magnifying the scope of mind. *See also* Shingon.

kengyō: The expressed teaching; exoteric teaching. Teachings that can be understood by ordinary people, expressed through standard language and logic. Contrasted with the Esoteric, or *mikkyō* teachings, typified by those of the Shingon school. *See also* Esoteric; *mikkyō;* Shingon.

kṣatriya: A member of the military or ruling class, the second of the four castes. *See also* four castes.

lunar mansion (Skt. *nakṣatra*): Twenty-seven or twenty-eight divisions of the sky, each identified by a prominent star or asterism, through which the moon passes during its monthly cycle. From ancient times China followed the system of twenty-eight lunar mansions, while in India the systems of twenty-seven (in which the lunar mansion Abhijit, called Ox in China, is omitted) and twenty-eight lunar mansions were both known. There is some debate about which system is older; the *Mātaṅga Sutra* shows evidence of both systems.

mahā-sukha: Lit., "great enjoyment," "supreme bliss." It refers to the great bliss generated by the union of male and female energies in tantric doctrine.

Mahāvairocana ("Great Sun"): The Buddha who is the central teacher and object of veneration in the Vajrayāna tradition. Mahāvairocana is the transcendent and cosmocratic apotheosis of the historical buddha, Śākyamuni. Under the earlier designation of Vairocana ("Luminous One"), he represents Buddhism's most profound speculation on the emptiness and interpenetration of all elements in the universe (Skt. *dharmadhātu*). As Mahāvairocana he is concretely envisaged as the all-encompassing lord of the cosmos and is the object of worship in a form of tantric Buddhism that spread from India to Sumatra, China, Japan, and Tibet. Originally the name referred to the light of the sun, but later on took on connotations of the buddha as fundamental principle of the universe. *See also dharmadhātu;* Vajrayāna.

Mahāvairocanābhisaṃbodhi-sūtra: A Mahayana sutra; the Chinese translation by Śubhākarasiṃha, with the assistance of Yixing, in 724 became the most important text for the East Asian Vajrayāna/Tantrayāna school. This scripture presents the world as a stage on which Vairocana reveals the three mysteries of the Esoteric tradition by which one may discover one's innate pure mind of enlightenment. This theme is addressed in the opening dialogue between Mahāvairocana and an assembly led by the bodhisattva Vajrapāṇi, who inquires about omniscience (*sarvajñajñāna*). The Bhagavān responds that it is caused by the mind that seeks enlightenment, is founded on compassion for others, and culminates in skillful means. *See also* Esoteric tradition; Mahāvairocana; three mysteries; Vajrapāṇi; Vajrayāna.

Mahayana ("Great Vehicle"): The name attached to a late Indian sectarian movement that became the main form of Buddhism in East Asia. The term was created together with the disparaging term Hinayana ("Lesser Vehicle"), which was used by the former to distinguish itself from the early Buddhist teaching (referred to as the Theravāda). In the polemical sense, the concept of a "great vehicle" refers to the fact that the Mahayana considered its doctrines to be more open and universal in advocating that enlightenment is attainable by all sentient beings, rather than only by monastics who practice in the pure environment of the monastery. This movement produced a large body of new sutras, in which the new model practitioner, the bodhisattva, preached the doctrine of the emptiness of all things. *See also* bodhisattva.

mantra (Jp. *shingon,* lit., "true word"): A mystical short verse or verbal formula to be recited that contains the power to bring about spiritual or temporal results. Originally in Indian Brahmanical religion, a syllable, word, or verse that was revealed to a seer while in meditation; thus, syllables recited during certain meditative practice; a power-laden syllable or series of syllables that manifests certain cosmic forces and aspects of the Buddha. In the Esoteric tradition a specific mantra is attributed to each deity for identification. *See also dhāraṇī;* Esoteric tradition.

Mātaṅga: A member of a certain hill tribe and, by extension, an outcaste; also used interchangeably with *caṇḍāla. See also caṇḍāla.*

mikkyō (Jp. "esoteric teachings"): The name of the Esoteric tradition in Japan. Also known as the Shingon school. *See also* Esoteric tradition; Shingon.

mudrā: Generally, this term refers to the hand gesture (seal) called *hasta-mudrā.* According to Esoteric tradition there are four kinds of s: (1) *mahā-mudrā* ("great seal"), (2) *samaya-mudrā* ("pledge seal"), (3) *dharma-mudrā* ("seal of the universal law that governs human existence"), which refers to the visualization of the seed letters (*bīja*) symbolizing the Buddha's teachings and ideal realm through formation; and (4) *karma-mudrā* ("action seal"). In the *Prajñāpāramitānaya-sūtra* (T. 243) *mudrā* refers to the *hasta-mudrā,* the hand gesture used to symbolize the nature and power/action of a particular deity. *See also bīja;* Esoteric tradition.

nāga: A class of serpentlike beings; usually rendered in Chinese as "dragon."

Nāgārjuna (second-third centuries C.E.): One of the most esteemed figures in Buddhist history, considered by many Mahayanists as second in insight and importance only to Buddha himself. A master of Sanskrit grammar and linguistics as well as a skilled debater and critical thinker, his masterwork, the *Mūlamadhyamaka-kārikā* (*Fundamental Verses on the Middle Way*), sharply critiqued with elegant, sophisticated verse many treasured concepts and theories held by Buddhists and non-Buddhists, from causality and time to karma and nirvana.

nirmāṇakāya: "transformation body"; the temporal body of the Buddha; the transformation of the Buddha's body into the form of a sentient being in order to teach and save them. One of the three bodies (*trikāya*) of the Buddha. *See also* three bodies.

pāda: Lit., "step, pace, footstep" in Sanskrit. In the *Prajñāpāramitānaya-sūtra* it means "in the state of." In the Chinese version of this text it is described as "word" rather than "step," "state of," but this is an apparent confusion with the term *padārtha,* "word" or "principle."

prajñāpāramitā: "Perfection of wisdom." Literally, to "reach the other shore" (nirvana) through wisdom. It also refers to the path of the perfection of wisdom emphasized repeatedly in the *Prajñāpāramitānaya-sūtra.*

Prasenajit: The king of Kośala. A contemporary of Śākyamuni, he ascended the throne in the same year that Śākyamuni attained enlightenment and, together with his wife and son, became a devout follower and patron of the Buddha.

pratyekabuddha: Solitary realizer, self-enlightened one, individual illuminate, etc. One who lives apart from others and attains enlightenment for himself, in contrast to the altruism of the bodhisattva principle. One of two paths of practice collectively referred to as the two vehicles. *See also* bodhisattva; two vehicles.

pūjā (Jp. *kuyō*): Worship, ritual offerings, and devotional rites to a deity.

ratna: Lit., "treasures, jewels," the term also connotes "value" and "richness." In the Shingon tradition it refers to the symbol of something beneficial, a productive/meritorious nature or power. In the Vajradhātu Maṇḍala it is depicted and located in the southern quadrant.

samādhi (Jp. *sanmaji*): Trance, mental concentration. In practical usage it refers to the state of trance attained through mental concentration and visualization.

samaya: Vow, oath, awakening; the act of removing hindrance, sameness, and oneness with an objective.

saṃbhogakāya: "Reward body," also called body of bliss or body of recompense. The ideal body of a buddha that is produced upon entering buddhahood as the result of vows undertaken during the practices of the bodhisattva path. One of the three bodies (*trikāya*) of the Buddha. *See also* three bodies.

Shingon (Jp. "true word"): The Chinese translation of the Sanskrit term "mantra," this school can be considered the East Asian version of Mantrayāna/Tantrayāna/Vajrayāna, also known as the Esoteric tradition. The formation of the school in China was based largely on scriptures brought to China by Śubhākarasiṃha, Vajrabodhi, and his disciple Amoghavajra. *See also* Amoghavajra; Esoteric tradition; *mikkyō.*

siddhi: Obtaining a power, accomplishing the ultimate goal, fulfillment, and achieving success in a particular spiritual mission.

six destinies: Six kinds of rebirth in samsara undergone by sentient beings in accord with their good or evil actions (karma) carried out in previous lifetimes. Beings are reborn into one of six realms of existence: (1) hell (Skt. *naraka-gati*), (2) hungry ghosts (*preta-gati*), (3) animals (*tiryagyoni-gati*), (4) titans (*asura-gati*), (5) humans (*manuṣya-gati*), and (6) gods (*deva-gati*).

śramaṇa/śramaṇā: An ascetic or religious mendicant (male and female, respectively).

śrāvaka: "Voice-hearer," a disciple. Originally, the term referred to a direct disciple of the Buddha, one who heard his teaching directly. In later Mahayana texts, it is used as a technical term with somewhat negative connotations. While *śrāvaka*s are disciplined monk-practitioners who contemplate the principle of the Four Noble Truths in order to attain arhatship, and thus eventually nirvana, they are also considered, along with the *pratyekabuddha,* to be practitioners of the two lesser vehicles, inferior in insight and compassion to the bodhisattva. *See also* arhat; bodhisattva; *pratyekabuddha;* two vehicles.

Śrāvastī: The capital of the kingdom of Kośala. *See also* Prasenajit.

śūdra: A member of the serf class, the lowest of the four castes. *See also* four castes.

surata (Jp. *byōteki*): Delightful ecstasy or pleasure attained through sexual intercourse. In the *Prajñāpāramitānaya-sūtra* it serves as a metaphor or allusion to express the state of great enjoyment (*mahā-sukha*) in the form of love in mutual interaction. *See also mahā-sukha.*

tathāgata (Jp. *nyorai*): Lit., one who has come (*āgata*) and gone (*gata*) beyond; an epithet of a buddha. In the *Prajñāpāramitānaya-sūtra* a tathāgata is also referred to as the Lord or a preacher who delivers the Dharma to his assembly, embodying the truth of suchness.

tathāgatagarbha: Lit., "matrix/womb (*garbha*) of the thus-come one (tathāgata)." This term refers to the capacity for becoming a tathāgata (i.e., enlightened) that is present in the minds of unenlightened sentient beings.

ten stages of faith: The first ten stages (*bhūmi*) in the fifty-two–stage path of the bodhisattva, so called because faith is the entry to Buddhist practice. *See also* bodhisattva.

three mysteries (Jp. *sanmitsu*): The three mystic modes of activity through body, speech, and mind, referring to the consecrating power of Mahāvairocana. Esoteric tradition practitioners seek to realize their buddha-nature through the performance of physical signs and postures (*mudrā*), the recitation of mantra and *dhāraṇī* (speech), and the practice of meditation, abiding in the state of *samādhi* (mind). See also buddha-nature; mantra; *dhāraṇī;* Mahāvairocana; *mudrā; samādhi.*

three poisons: The three basic afflictions: desire or craving (*rāga*); anger or ill-will (*dveṣa*); and delusion or ignorance (*moha*).

three vehicles: The three paths (Skt. *triyāna*) of practice of *śrāvakas*, *pratyekabuddhas*, and bodhisattvas. As taught in the Mahayana schools, these three paths of practice are considered to be suitable for different capacities of sentient beings, with the first two vehicles categorized by the Mahayana as the "Lesser Vehicle" (Hinayana). *See also* two vehicles.

triple realm (Jp. *sangai*): Also called the triple world, the three levels of samsara into which sentient beings are reborn: the realm of desire (or delusion) (*kāmadhātu*), the realm of form (*rūpadhātu*), and the formless realm (*ārūpyadhātu*), the inhabitants of which have no physical bodies.

twelve-stage causation (Skt. *pratītyasamutpāda*): The core Buddhist teaching that all phenomena arise from conditions: nothing arises out of nothing, nothing arises of itself, and things do not come into existence through the power of an external creator. There is nothing that is self-contained, independent, or that has its own separate and independent nature. Twelve-stage causation is the condition of relationship to something else resulting in arising or production.

two vehicles: The vehicles of the *śrāvaka*s ("voice-hearers," direct disciples) and *pratyeka-buddha*s (self-realizers). These two kinds of practitioners are regularly mentioned in Mahayana literature, generally cast in a negative light as representatives of the so-called Hinayana ("Lesser Vehicle") tradition, in contradistinction to the bodhisattva path of the Mahayana. They are understood as practitioners who are engaged in a view toward practice and enlightenment that will lead to attainment of arhatship but not buddhahood. *See also* arhat; Mahayana; *pratyekabuddha; śrāvaka.*

vaiśya: A member of the class of peasants, merchants, and artisans, the third of the four castes. *See also* four castes.

vajra (Jp. *kongō*): Diamondlike, adamantine, imperishable/immovable nature. The term connotes wisdom, enlightenment, the Buddha's power, and in practical terms refers to the thunderbolt-shaped ritual implements, of which there are three types: the single-pronged *vajra* (Jp. *tokko-sho*), the three-pronged *vajra* (Jp. *sanko-sho*), and the five-pronged *vajra* (Jp. *goko-sho*). These types of implements derive from weapons used in ancient India.

Vajrapāṇi (Jp. Kongōshu): A great bodhisattva generally equated with Vajrasattva Bodhisattva, an ideal being in the Mahayana Buddhist tradition, one who seeks enlightenment through the salvation of all sentient beings. In the Esoteric tradition he is portrayed and symbolized in the form of great desire, physical contact, love, and mastery in love.

Bibliography

Astley-Kristensen, Ian. "An Annotated Translation of Amoghavajra's Commentary on the *Liqu jing* (*Rishukyō*)—Part I," *Studies in Central and East Asian Religions* 7 (1994): 27–53.

—. *The Rishukyō: The Sino-Japanese Tantric Prajñāpāramitā in 150 Verses—Amoghavajra's Version.* Buddhica Britannica, vol. 3. Tring, UK: Institute of Buddhist Studies, 1991.

Kiyota, Minoru, ed. *Mahayana Buddhist Meditation: Theory and Practice.* Honolulu: University Press of Hawai'i, 1978.

—. *Shingon Buddhism: Theory and Practice.* Los Angeles: Buddhist Books International, 1978.

—. "Shingon Mikkyō's Twofold Maṇḍala: Paradoxes and Integration," *Journal of the International Association of Buddhist Studies* 10/1 (1987): 91–116.

—. *Tantric Concept of Bodhicitta: A Buddhist Experiential Philosophy (An Exposition Based upon the Mahā-Vairocana-Sutra, Bodhicitta-Śastra, and Sokushin-Jobutsu-Gi).* Madison, WI: South Asian Area Center, University of Wisconsin, 1982.

Miyasaka, Yūshō, ed. *Jōyō-Darani to Sho-shingon* (*Dhāraṇī and Mantra in Daily Use*). *Chizan Kyōka Shiryō,* vol. 4. Kyoto: Chishakuin Kenkyūsho, 2000, rev. ed.

Miyata, Taisen. *The Way of Great Enjoyment.* Los Angeles: Koyasan Betsuin Temple, 1996, rev. ed. A translation of the *Hannyarishu-kyō.*

Mukhopadhyaya, Sujitkumar, ed. *The Śārdūlakarṇāvadāna.* Santiniketan: Viśvabharati, 1954.

—. "A Critical Study of the *Śārdūlakarṇāvadāna* from the Brāhmaṇic Literary Sources," *Visva-Bharati Annals* 12/1 (1967): 1–108.

Sharma, Sharmishta. *Astrological Lore in the Buddhist Śārdūlakarṇāvadāna.* Delhi: Eastern Book Linkers, 1992.

Takakusu, Junjirō, and Kaikyoku Watanabe, eds. *Banruo liqu shi jing* (*Commentary on the Banruo liqu jing*) by Amoghavajra (Bukong). In *Taishō shinshū daizōkyō,* vol. 19, no. 1003, p. 607. Tokyo: Taishō issaikyō kankōkai, 1924–1934.

Toganoo, Shōun. *Rishukyō no kenkyū* (*A Study of the Rishukyō*). Koyasan: Koyasan University Press, 1959.

—. *Wabun Kyōten: Hannyarishukyō* (*Hannyarishukyō in Modern Japanese*). Koyasan: Koyasan Shuppansha, 1973.

White, Kenneth R. *Bodhicitta in Kūkai's Shingon Practice.* Madison, WI: University of Wisconsin–Madison, 1998.

—. *The Role of Bodhicitta in Buddhist Enlightenment Including a Translation into English of Bodhicitta-Sastra, Benkemmitsu-Nikyoron, and Sammaya-Kaijo.* Lewiston, NY: Edwin Mellen Press, 2005.

Index

A

adhiṣṭhāna. See empower/empowered/ empowerment
Agnidatta (Fire-given), 46
Ākāśagarbha, 11, 16, 25n7
Akṣobhya, 120
Amitābha/Amitāyus, 25n6, 120, 121
  See also five budddhas
Amitāyurdhyāna-sūtra, 116
Amoghasiddhi, 120, 121
Amoghavajra, 5, 6, 9, 25n12, 105, 107
Ānanda, 31
  and Prakṛti, 32, 33, 37–39, 40–42, 92
An Shigao, 31
arhat, 42, 43, 92
Arundhatī, 94n17
asterism, 32, 67–70, 74, 78, 82, 89, 91–92, 95n32, 96nn37, 38, 39; 97n45
  See also constellations; planets; star(s)
astrology/astronomy, 32, 33, 61, 65
  See also asterism; eclipse(s); constellations; lunar mansions, twenty-eight; planets; seven luminaries; stars
avadāna, 31, 32
Avalokiteśvara, 11, 15, 25n6
Avataṃsaka-sūtra, 105, 111, 116, 129n6
awakening, 13, 105
  of *bodhicitta,* 106, 107, 117
  See also bodhi; enlightenment

B

Banruo liqu jing. See Hannyarishukyō
Bharadvāja, 59
Bhīma/Bhīsma, 53, 94n19
bhūmi. See stage(s)
bīja. See seed syllable(s)/syllable(s)
birth and death, 22, 38, 43, 48
bodhi, 105, 109, 122
  path to, 55
  practices, 109
  seat, 12, 14
  supreme, 115, 116, 119, 123
  See also awakening; enlightenment
bodhicitta, 18, 105, 106, 107, 109–110, 114, 117, 119, 121, 122, 123, 125, 126–127
  See also enlightenment, mind/thought of
Bodhicitta-śāstra, 105–106, 107
bodhisattva(s) 5, 11, 12, 20, 22, 23, 24, 110, 114, 120–121
practice(s), 21, 105, 114, 125
  stage(s), 115, 123
  vajra-holder, 13, 23
  See also eight *pūjā*-bodhisattvas; four *saṃgraha*-bodhisattvas; four *pāramitā*-bodhisattvas; sixteen *mahā*-bodhisattvas
bodies, of buddha(s)/tathāgata(s), 16, 109, 116, 125, 126
  dharmakāya (truth body), 126
  nirmāṇakāya (historically transformed body), 126
  niṣyandakāya (body that enters the six destinies), 126

bodies, of buddha(s)/tathāgata(s) (*continued*):
  saṃbhogakāya (means body), 126
  vajra-body, 123
Brahmā, 40, 41, 47, 50–51, 52, 57, 58, 62, 63
brahman(s)/brahmanical, 32, 41, 45, 46–47, 48–53, 56, 57, 58, 61, 64, 68, 70, 73, 79, 85, 86, 87, 89, 90, 92, 94nn11, 21, 95n23
  See also caste(s), four; clans
Buddha, 12, 21, 24, 26n14, 31, 32, 37, 38, 40, 45, 55, 57, 61, 67, 92, 114, 123, 125, 126
  and Ānanda, 40–41
  body of, 116, 125, 126
  historical, 105
  and Prakṛti, 41–43, 45
  teaching(s), 16, 115
  wisdom, 116, 122, 127
  See also Gautama; Śākyamuni; Tathāgata
buddha(s), 20, 110, 114, 115, 116, 119–121, 125, 126
  -cognitions, 120
  five, 119–120, 121
  fruit, 114
  land, 127
  -mind, 116
  practices, 116
  stage, 126
  vehicle, 26, 109
buddhahood, 11, 115, 125
  five stages to realization of, 123
  in the present body, 110
buddha-nature, 111
  See also tathāgatagarbha
Buddhism/Buddhist, 5, 6, 7, 105
  See also esoteric/Esoteric Buddhist tradition
Bukong. *See* Amoghavajra

C

cakra. *See* wheel
cakravartin. *See* wheel-turning sage-king
caṇḍāla(s), *caṇḍāla-mātaṅga*, 32, 33, 37–41, 45–48, 52, 53
  See also caste(s); outcaste
caste(s), 32, 49, 50, 51, 53, 55, 56, 59
  four, 50–51, 94n11, 95n26
  See also brahman(s); *caṇḍāla*(s); *kṣatriya*(s); outcaste; *śūdra*(s); *vaiśya*(s)
Chang'an, 6, 9
China, 6, 9, 97n49, 129
Chinese, 5, 6, 9, 31, 32, 33, 93nn1, 2, 4, 5, 6, 8; 94n16, 95nn27, 29, 31; 96nn33, 34, 36, 37, 39; 97nn40, 43, 46, 49; 98nn50, 53, 55, 56, 60; 99nn61, 62, 63; 105, 129n3
clans (*gotra*), 56, 58, 59, 62, 63, 64, 80, 81, 95nn25, 32; 96n33, 116
  Ālambāyana, 63
  Ātreya, 58, 95n29
  Aupamanyava, 62
  Bhāradvāja, 62
  Bhārgava, 64
  Brahman, 63
  Caitrāyaṇa, 62
  Calf (Vātsya), 56
  Deer (Mṛgāyaṇa), 62
  Dragon, 62
  Drāhyāyaṇa, 64
  Eight Beauties (Aṣṭabhaginīya), 64
  Gautama, 56
  Good, 62
  Jātūkarṇya, 64
  Kālāyana, 63
  Kāśyapa, 56
  Kātyāyana, 63
  Kauṇḍinyāyana, 63
  Kauśika, 56
  Kautsa, 56

Māṇḍavya, 56
Dhaumrāyaṇa, 95n25
Pārāśarīya, 59
Piṅgalāyana, 62
Red, 63
Saṃcayana, 63
Settled (Hāritāyanīya), 62, 96n33
Śyāmāyana, 62
Tāṇḍyāyana, 63
Tvaṣṭṛ, 62, 63
Vaiśyāyana, 62
Vāsiṣṭha (Vāśiṣṭha), 56
See also lunar mansions, twenty-eight
cognition(s), 115, 120, 122, 129
buddha-, 120
seal of, 15, 16
constellations, 61, 67, 92
See also asterism; lunar mansions, twenty-eight; planets; seven luminaries; stars
Cunda, 116

D

Daguangzhi, 107, 109
See also Amoghavajra
Dale jingang pukong zhenshi san moheye jing. See Prajñāpāramitānaya-sūtra
Daxingshan Monastery/Daxingshansi Temple, 9, 107
delusion, 111, 115, 119
demon(s), 22, 38, 41
dharma(s), 11, 12, 13, 14, 15, 21, 113, 114, 115, 122, 125, 126
equality/sameness of, 14, 15, 18, 19, 21, 22, 23
Dharma, 11, 12, 13, 16, 20, 24, 37, 42, 43, 92, 106, 110, 111, 113, 114, 115, 116, 120, 126
eye, 92
of the four truths, 42, 113
-nature, 13, 16, 19, 20, 22
of non-Buddhists, 109, 113
wheel, 11, 17, 18, 115, 120
dharmadhātu, 106, 119, 120, 123
Dharmadhātu/Dharmakāya Mahāvairocana, 105, 106, 120
See also Mahāvairocana
dharmakāya. See bodies, of buddha(s)/tathāgata(s)
Dharma Mantra, 110, 126
See also mantra
Dharmarakṣa, 31, 33
Dharma Samādhi, 110
See also samādhi
Divyāvadāna, 31
Dove-seeker, 52, 94n15
Drink (Pāna?), 52
Dvaipāyana, 53, 94n18
See also Vyāsa

E

eclipse(s), 73–74, 97n40
eight *pūjā*-bodhisattvas:
Vajradhūpā, 121
Vajragandhā, 121
Vajragītā, 121
Vajralāsyā, 121
Vajrālokā, 121
Vajramālā, 121
Vajranṛityā, 121
Vajrapuṣpā, 121
element(s), 82, 97n45
four, 79, 113
three, 79, 82, 97n44, 45
empower/empowered/empowerment, 11, 16, 20, 21, 23, 24
emptiness, 105, 106, 121, 125
of *dharma*s, 115
of self/self-nature, 105, 121
enlightenment, 5, 6, 13, 19, 25n9, 26n17, 105, 106, 110, 111, 116, 119, 122, 125, 126

enlightenment (*continued*):
four phases of, 14, 25n4
great, 13, 22, 119, 127
initial, 116, 117
mind/thought of, 18, 25n3, 122
perfect/unsurpassed, 13, 14, 15, 17
supreme, 105, 107, 109, 111, 122
See also awakening; *bodhi*
eon(s), 55, 56, 57, 114
asaṃkhyeya, 45, 57
See also kalpa
esoteric/Esoteric Buddhist tradition, 5, 6, 7, 25n11
See also Mantra Dharma; Shingon; tantric
exoteric, 105, 125
evil destinies, 14, 155
See also six destinies

F

faculties, 109
supernatural, five, 52, 53, 57
five aggregates, 113
five buddhas. *See* buddha(s), five
flower(s), 12, 38, 39, 41, 45, 46, 50, 53, 62, 63, 68, 69, 72, 73, 75, 77, 87, 88
arka, 38
atimuktaka, 50
campaka, 50
peach, 62, 63
sumanā, 50
utpala, 50
See also lotus
four groups of practitioners, 45, 92
Four Heavenly Kings, 40
four (noble) truths. *See* truth(s), four
four *pāramitā*-bodhisattvas, 120, 121
Dharma-pāramitā, 120
Karma-pāramitā, 120
Ratna-pāramitā, 120
Vajra-pāramitā, 120
four *saṃgraha*-bodhisattvas, 121
Vajrāṅkuśa, 121
Vajrapāśa, 121
Vajrasphoṭa, 121
Vajrāveśa, 121
Four Sisters, 21, 26n17

G

Gaganagañja, 11, 18
*gandharva*s, 38
Ganges River, 45
gardens/groves/parks, 45, 46–47, 77
Anāthapiṇḍada's Garden, 37
Atimukta, 45
Jeta's Grove, 37, 40, 41, 45
Nandana, 47, 93n9
Sumanaska (Happy), 46
Gautama, 38, 40, 41–42, 56
See also Buddha; Śākyamuni
Gāyatrī, 95n26
god(s), 38, 41, 47, 58, 62–64, 68, 75, 78, 79, 87–89, 98n55, 109, 117
Āditya, 87
Agni (Fire), 62, 63, 87
Ahirbudhnya, 64
Āpas, 88
Bhaga, 62
Bhava, 62, 64
Ferocious God, 63
Jupiter, 62, 65, 87, 91
Kitchen God, 88
Mitra, 63
Mountain God, 88
Pitṛ, 62
Prajāpati (Fire), 87
Pūṣan, 64
Rudra, 87
Śada, 63
Sarpa, 62
Savitṛ, 58, 95n26
Soma, 62, 87

Sūrya, 62
Toya, 63
Tvaṣṭṛ, 62, 63
Varuṇa, 63, 88
Vasu, 57, 63
Viṣṇu, 63, 94n20
Yama, 64
See also Brahmā; Indra; Rāma; Śakra Devendra
Good Path, 52
Great Vehicle, 13, 24
See also Mahayana; vehicle(s)

H

Hannyarishukyō, 5–6
See also Prajñāpāramitānaya-sūtra
Happy (Nandaka), 51
Hayashiya, Tomojirō, 31
Himalayas. *See* Snowy Mountains
Hindu/Hinduism, 94n19, 95n26, 96n38
Huayan jing. See Avataṃsaka-sūtra
human-buddha integration, 105–106
See also buddhahood, in the present body; *sokushin jōbutsu*

I

India/Indian, 5, 6, 31, 35, 97nn44, 49; 98nn51, 60; 99n61
Indo-Scythian, 31
Indra, 63, 93n9, 97nn44, 45

J

Jamadagni, 53, 94n20
Japan/Japanese, 5, 6, 7, 31, 105, 106
Jin, Eastern/Western, 31
Joyous, 51
See also Śatāyus

K

Kāleya, 58, 95n30
Kāliṅga, 97n41
kalpa(s), 114, 125
See also eon
Kapilā (Yellow Head), 57
karma/karmic, 12, 14, 16, 18, 20, 32, 41, 43, 51, 113, 125
Kauravas, 94n19
Kautsya (Oftentimes), 59
kengyō. See exoteric
knowledge, 19, 23, 33, 46, 52, 99n61, 109, 116
of all-knowledge, 126
of all particulars/phenomena, 16, 111, 123
discriminatory, 17
nondiscriminatory, 25n9
spontaneous, 111
unobstructed, 111, 116
Kōbō Daishi, 6
See also Kūkai
Kongōsatta. *See* sixteen *māha*-bodhisattvas, Vajrasattva
Kōyasan Shingon Mission, 7
kṣatriya(s), 50, 51, 53, 56, 58, 94n11, 95nn22, 26
See also caste(s)
Kūkai, 6, 106
Kumārajīva, 129
Kurukṣetra, 94n19

L

Laws of Manu, 93n10
layman/laymen, laywomen, 31, 40, 91
Longevous (Jīvaka), 51
lotus(es), 14, 15, 23, 50, 122, 125
Lotus Sutra, 122
lunar mansions (*nakṣatra*), twenty-eight, 32, 61–65, 67–70, 73–74, 76–82, 87–91, 95nn31, 32; 96nn33, 34, 36, 37; 97nn40, 43; 98n60
Astride (Revatī), 61, 64, 68, 70, 73, 74, 78, 82, 88, 89, 90, 92

lunar mansions (*continued*):
Base (Viśākhā), 61, 63, 64, 67, 69, 72, 74, 77, 81, 88, 89, 91, 92
Cross Board of a Carriage (Hastā), 62, 67, 69, 71, 74, 76, 80, 81, 88, 89, 91, 96n35
Dipper (Uttarāṣāḍhā), 61, 63, 64, 68, 69, 72, 74, 77, 78, 81, 88, 89, 92
Drawn Bow (Pūrvaphalgunī), 61, 62, 64, 67, 69, 71, 74, 76, 80, 87, 89, 91
Ghost (Puṣya), 61, 62, 64, 67, 68, 71, 72, 75, 80, 87, 89, 90, 91, 99n63
Heart (Jyeṣṭhā), 61, 63, 64, 67, 69, 72, 74, 77, 81, 88, 89, 91, 92
Horn (Citrā), 61, 62, 64, 67, 69, 71, 74, 76, 81, 88, 89, 90, 91
House (Pūrvabhādrapada), 61, 63–64, 68, 69, 70, 73, 74, 78, 81, 88, 89, 90, 92
Mound (Aśvinī), 61, 64, 68, 70, 73, 74, 78, 82, 88, 89, 90, 92, 97n42
Neck (Svātī), 61, 63, 64, 67, 69, 71, 74, 76, 81, 88, 89, 90, 91
Net (Rohiṇī), 61, 64, 67, 68, 70, 73, 75, 80, 87, 89, 91
Orion (Ārdrā), 61, 62, 64, 67, 68, 70, 73, 75, 80, 87, 89, 91
Ox (Abhijit), 61, 63, 64, 68, 74, 78, 89, 92, 96n37, 97n43, 98n58
Pleiades (Kṛttikā), 61, 62, 64, 67, 68, 70, 73, 74, 80, 87, 89, 90, 91, 92, 96n38
Rooftop (Śatabhiṣaj), 61, 63–64, 68, 69, 72, 74, 78, 81, 88, 89, 90, 92
Room (Anurādhā), 61, 63, 64, 67, 69, 72, 74, 77, 81, 88, 89, 90, 92
Seven Stars (Maghā), 61, 62, 64, 67, 68, 71, 74, 76, 80, 87, 89, 90, 91
Stomach (Bharaṇī), 61, 64, 68, 70, 73, 74, 79, 82, 89, 90, 92
Tail (Mūlā), 61, 63, 64, 67, 69, 72, 74, 77, 81, 88, 89, 92
Turtle (Mṛgaśiras), 61, 62, 64, 67, 68, 70, 73, 74, 75, 80, 87, 89, 90, 91, 92, 96n35
Void (Dhaniṣṭhā), 61, 63, 64, 68, 69, 72, 74, 78, 81, 88, 89, 92
Wall (Uttarabhādrapada), 61, 64, 68, 70, 73, 74, 78, 82, 88, 89, 92
Well (Punarvasu), 61, 62, 64, 67, 68, 71, 73, 75, 80, 87, 89, 91
Willow (Aśleṣā), 61, 62, 64, 67, 68, 71, 73, 75, 80, 87, 89, 91
Wing (Uttaraphalgunī), 61, 62, 64, 67, 69, 71, 74, 76, 80, 87, 89, 90, 91
Winnowing Basket (Pūrvāṣāḍhā), 61, 63, 64, 68, 69, 72, 74, 77, 81, 88, 89, 90, 91, 92
Woman (Śravaṇā), 61, 63, 64, 68, 69, 70, 72, 74, 78, 81, 88, 89, 90, 92

M

Madhukāra, 21
See also Three Brothers
Magadha, 97n41
Mahābhārata, 94nn18, 19
mahābodhi. See enlightenment, great
Mahāsukhavajra-amoghasamaya-sūtra. See Prajñāpāramitānaya-sūtra
Mahāvairocana, 5, 11, 23, 25n4, 105, 106, 109, 120, 121, 126
Dharmadhātu/Dharmakāya, 105, 106, 120
See also Vairocana
Mahāvairocanābhisaṃbodhi-sūtra/ Mahāvairocanā-sūtra, 115, 117, 121, 122, 125, 126, 129n1
Mahayana, 106, 114
panjiao system of text classification, 129n3
See also Great Vehicle

Maheśvara, 20
maṇḍala(s), 13, 109
maṇi jewels, 11
Mañjuśrī, 11, 17, 25n9
mantra(s), 5, 6, 25nn11, 12; 93n4, 123
  heart-, 21
  oṃ maṇi padme hūṃ, 93n4
  practitioner, 111–114, 119, 126
  vajra-hūm-kara (wrathful), 15
  See also spell
Mantra Dharma, 110, 126
  See also esoteric/Esoteric Buddhist tradition
Māra(s), 22, 24, 109
Mātaṅga(s)/Mātaṅgī(s), 32, 33, 46, 47, 48, 92
Mātaṅga Sutra, 31–33, 35, 65, 92
Mātaṅgī-sūtra. See Mātaṅga Sutra
meditation, 52, 57, 68, 119, 121, 123, 125, 126
  methods/techniques, 56, 57
  on the moon, 119
  on the syllable *"A,"* 122–123
merit(s)/meritorious, 5, 13, 23, 25nn7, 8; 47, 55, 57, 77, 78, 82, 92, 107, 109
mikkyō. See esoteric/Esoteric Buddhist tradition
monk(s), 6, 31, 37, 38, 39, 40, 42, 45, 92
mudrā(s), 5, 6, 11, 16, 17, 120, 123
  of conquering the triple realm (*trailokyavijayarāja*), 14
  samaya vajra fist, 17
  of *vajra*-hooking, 26n15
  "wisdom fist," 14

N

nāga(s), 57, 73, 80, 91
Nāgārjuna, 105
nirvana, 5, 23, 25nn8, 12; 55, 114, 122
Nirvāṇa-sūtra, 116
non-Buddhist(s), 109, 113, 114
no-self, 116
nun(s), 32, 33, 40, 42, 45, 92

O

outcaste, 31, 32, 33
  See also caṇḍāla(s); caste(s)

P

Pāṇḍava brothers, five, 94n19
  See also Mahābhārata
Paranirmitavaśavartin, 11
Parāśara, 53
Paraśurāma, 94n20
  See also Rāma
Payne, Richard K., 7
perfection(s), 16, 17, 21, 22, 23, 119, 122, 126
  six, 114
  of wisdom, 12, 13, 14, 15, 16, 17, 18, 19, 20, 21, 22, 23
  See also prajñāpāramitā
planets, 65
  Ketu (Comet), 65
  Rāhu, 65
  See also constellations; lunar mansions, twenty-eight; seven luminaries; stars
power(s), 16, 20, 22, 38, 40–41, 46, 47, 95n22, 116
  supernatural, 40, 53
prajñāpāramitā, 12, 14, 15, 17, 18, 19–20, 21
  See also perfection, of wisdom
Prajñāpāramitānaya-sūtra, 5–6, 9
  See also Hannyarishukyō
Prakṛti (Original Nature), 31–33, 37, 45, 46, 92, 93n1
Prasenajit, King, 32, 38, 45, 92
pratītyasamutpāda. See twelve-stage causation
pratyekabuddha(s), 109, 113, 114, 117

precepts, 39, 42, 46, 48, 49, 55, 67, 68, 75, 80
Pure (Śuddha?), 52
Puruṣa, 94
Puṣkarasārin (Lotus-flower Essence), 32, 46–48, 50, 55, 57, 58, 61, 73, 92
See also Śāriputra
Puṣya, 52

R

Rāma, 53, 94n20
Rāmāyaṇa, 94n20
Ratnasaṃbhava, 120
Reṇukā (Dust Mote), 53, 94n20
Rishu-bō, 6

S

Sacittotpādadharmacakrapravartin, 11, 18
sādhana, 6
Śakra Devendra, 40, 47, 57, 88
Śākyamuni, 14, 40, 105
See also Buddha, historical; Gautama
salvation, 5, 18, 25nn3, 8; 111, 112,113
samādhi(s), 110, 119, 125
of all the tathāgatas, 16, 20
of the equality of all *dharma*s, 13
Samādhi Dharma, 110
samaya, 11, 17, 19
See also vow
Samantabhadra, 20, 119, 125
Sanskrit, 6, 25nn1–2, 31–33; 93nn1–3, 5, 8; 94nn12, 15–16, 18, 20–21; 95nn23–25, 27–28, 31; 96nn33–39; 97nn41–42, 46, 48–49; 98nn50, 52–60; 99nn61–62
Śārdūlakarṇa (Lion's Ear), 32, 33, 46, 48, 92, 93n6
See also Ānanda
Śārdūlakarṇāvadāna, 31, 97n49
Śāriputra, 92
Sarvamārapramardin, 11, 19
Sarvārthasiddha, 126
Sarvavinayasamartha, 19
śāstra(s), 105, 106
Śatāyus, 94n12
See also Joyous
Satyavatī, 94n18
Sāvitrī, 95n26
See also Gāyatrī; spell, Sāvitra
seed syllable(s)/syllable(s), 5, 6, 25nn3–6, 8–9, 11, 13; 26nn14, 16–18; 57, 95n26, 122–123
A, 122–123
Ā, 122
aḥ/AḤ, 17, 25n8, 122
āh/ĀH, 14, 25n4, 122
aṃ/AṂ, 17, 25n9, 122
hah, 19
ham, 21, 26n17
hum, 15, 25n5
hūṃ, 13, 18, 20, 23, 25nn3, 10, 13; 26n18
hrīh, 15, 25n6
oṃ, 18, 25n11, 58
svā, 21, 26n16
trām, 16, 25n7
trī, 20, 26n14
self/self-nature, 12, 14, 15, 17, 20, 56, 58, 105, 113, 114, 115, 116, 121, 126
six sense fields, organs, 121
Seven Deva/Heavenly Mothers, 20–21
seven luminaries, 65, 91
Jupiter (Bṛhaspati), 62, 65, 87, 91
Mars, 65, 91
Mercury, 65, 91
moon, 32, 47, 48, 49, 51, 61–65, 67–79, 80–82, 85, 87–91, 95n32, 96nn34, 36, 38; 97nn40, 45; 98n60, 105, 119, 121, 123
sixteen phases of, 105, 121
Saturn, 65, 91
sun, 47, 51, 53, 62, 65, 82, 85, 87, 91, 95n26, 99n61, 119, 121

Venus, 65, 91
See also asterism; planets; stars
Shingon, 5, 6, 25n6, 105, 106
See also esoteric/Esoteric Buddhist tradition
six destinies, 115, 121, 125, 126
sixteen *mahā*-bodhisattvas:
Vajrabhāṣa, 121
Vajradaṃṣṭra, 121
Vajradharma, 121
Vajrahāsā, 120
Vajrahetu, 121
Vajrakarma, 121
Vajraketu, 120
Vajraprabha, 120
Vajrarāja, 120
Vajrarakṣa, 121
Vajraratna, 120
Vajrasādhu, 120
Vajrasaṃdhi, 119, 121
Vajrasattva, 5, 25n3, 26n18, 119, 120
Vajratīkṣṇa, 121
Vajravāśin, 120
skandhas. *See* five aggregates
skillful means/skill-in-means, 23, 112, 114, 116, 117, 119, 120
Snowy Mountains, 47
sokushin jōbutsu, 105, 106, 110
See also buddhahood, in the present body; human-buddha integration
Sorrowless (Aśoka), 51
spell(s), 32, 37, 38, 39–41, 49, 57–58, 93nn2–5
Sāvitra, 57, 58, 95nn26, 27
six-phrase/six-syllable, 40, 99n4
See also mantra; *Sāvitrī*
śramaṇa, 37, 38, 40, 41, 42
śrāvaka(s), 109, 113, 114, 117
Śrāvastī, 32, 37, 41
stage(s), 5, 105, 114, 123
bodhisattva/buddha, 115, 126
fifty-three, 105
first/of joy, 116, 123
five, of awakening, 105, 123
of ordinary person, 116, 126
ten, of faith, 114
stars, 32, 47, 49, 61–64, 70, 82, 86, 95n32
See also asterism; constellations; planets; seven luminaries
Sudhanaśreṣṭhi-dāraka, 105
śūdra(s), 50, 51, 56, 58, 94n11
See also caste(s)
Śuka (Parrot), 52
śūnyatā. *See* emptiness
supernatural, 40
faculties, five, 52, 53, 57
power(s), 40, 53
Śūraṅgama-sūtra, 31
Svabhāvaśuddha. *See* Avalokiteśvara
Śvetaketu (White-pure; Pure Cover), 52, 57

T

Tagore, Rabindranath, 32
Chandalika, 32
Takṣaka, 57
tantric, 105, 106
See also esoteric/Esoteric Buddhist tradition
tathāgata(s), 11, 13, 15, 16, 17, 18, 19, 20, 21, 22, 23, 24
Tathāgata, 15, 16, 17, 18, 19, 20, 21, 39, 42, 111, 116, 123, 126
See also Buddha; Śākyamuni
tathāgatagarbha, 20, 106, 111
See also buddha-nature
Three Brothers, 21, 26n16
three mysteries, 123, 126
Tibetan, 31, 32, 98n50
time, divisions of:
kalā, 86, 98n50
kāṣṭhā, 86, 98n50

time, divisions of (*continued*):
  kṣaṇa, 85, 978n48
  lava, 85, 86, 98n50
  muhūrta, 85–86, 90–91, 97nn46, 49
  nāḍikā, 86, 98n50
Toganoo, Shōun, 6–7
  Rishukyō no kenkyū (*A Study of the Rishukyō*), 6
  Wabun Kyōten: Hannyarishukyō (*Hannyarishukyō in Modern Japanese*), 7
Tripiṭaka, 9, 35, 107
triple realm/world, 11, 13, 14, 15, 16, 22, 23, 113, 114, 117
Triśaṅku, 32–33, 45–48, 50, 55, 57, 61, 62, 67, 73, 74, 92
truth(s), 43, 52, 55–56, 115, 126, 129n3
  four, 42, 113
  supreme (*paramārtha-satya*), 110, 113, 115, 123
Tumburu, 21
twelve-stage causation, 113

V

Vairocana, 11, 13, 22
  See also Mahāvairocana
vaiśya(s), 50, 51, 56, 58, 94n11
  See also caste(s)
vajra, 13, 15, 16, 17, 19, 20, 24, 120, 123
  cakra/wheel, 18
  -holder, 13, 23
  -hooking, 26n15
  -seat, 126
  Vajradhara, 23
Vajradhātu Maṇḍala, thirty-seven deities of, 119–121
Vajramusti, 11, 17
Vajrapāṇi, 11, 12–13, 14, 15, 16, 20, 21, 23, 24
Vajraśekhara-sūtra, 107, 126
Vajrayakṣa, 19, 25n12
Vasiṣṭha, 52, 94n17
Vātsya (Single), 59
Vedas, Vedic canons, four, 45, 46, 48, 51–53, 57, 94nn11, 16–17
  Apotropes (*Atharvaveda*), 52, 94n16
  Chants (*Sāmaveda*), 52, 94n16
  Hymns (*Ṛgveda*), 52, 94n16, 95nn26, 28
    "Hymn of Man" ("Puruṣa-sūkta"), 94n11
  Sacrifices (*Yajurveda*), 52, 94nn14, 16; 95n26
vehicle(s):
  buddha, 26, 109
  three, 125
  two, 109, 111, 113, 114, 125
  See also Great Vehicle
vow(s), 11, 13, 16, 17, 18, 19, 20, 21, 25n9, 53, 109, 110, 111, 115, 120, 125
  of fulfilling the great perpetual bliss, 13, 22, 23
  See also samaya
Vyāsa, 94n18
  See also Dvaipāyana

W

Wagner, Richard, 31
  Die Sieger (*The Victors*), 32
wheel, 17, 18
  of a letter (*akṣara-cakra*), 17
  vajra, 18
wheel-turning sage-king, 57
World-honored One, 39, 41–43
  See also Buddha; Tathāgata
Wu, kingdom, 31, 35

Y

Yangdu, 31
yoga, 109, 115, 119, 123
  -dhāraṇī, 107

Z

Zhi Qian, 31, 35
Zhu Lüyan, 31, 35

BDK English Tripiṭaka
(First Series)

Abbreviations

Ch.: Chinese
Skt.: Sanskrit
Jp.: Japanese
Eng.: Published title

Title		Taishō No.
Ch.	Chang ahan jing (長阿含經)	1
Skt.	Dīrghāgama	
Ch.	Zhong ahan jing (中阿含經)	26
Skt.	Madhyamāgama	
Eng.	*The Madhyama Āgama (Middle-length Discourses)* (Volume I, 2013)	
Ch.	Dasheng bensheng xindi guan jing (大乘本生心地觀經)	159
Ch.	Fo suoxing zan (佛所行讃)	192
Skt.	Buddhacarita	
Eng.	*Buddhacarita: In Praise of Buddha's Acts* (2009)	
Ch.	Zabao zang jing (雜寶藏經)	203
Eng.	*The Storehouse of Sundry Valuables* (1994)	
Ch.	Faju piyu jing (法句譬喩經)	211
Eng.	*The Scriptural Text: Verses of the Doctrine, with Parables* (1999)	
Ch.	Xiaopin banruo boluomi jing (小品般若波羅蜜經)	227
Skt.	Aṣṭasāhasrikā-prajñāpāramitā-sūtra	
Ch.	Jingang banruo boluomi jing (金剛般若波羅蜜經)	235
Skt.	Vajracchedikā-prajñāpāramitā-sūtra	
Ch.	Daluo jingang bukong zhenshi sanmoye jing (大樂金剛不空眞實三麼耶經)	243

Title		Taishō No.
Skt.	Adhyardhaśatikā-prajñāpāramitā-sūtra	
Eng.	*The Sutra of the Vow of Fulfilling the Great Perpetual Enjoyment and Benefiting All Sentient Beings Without Exception* (in *Esoteric Texts,* 2015)	
Ch.	Renwang banruo boluomi jing (仁王般若波羅蜜經)	245
Skt.	*Kāruṇikārājā-prajñāpāramitā-sūtra	
Ch.	Banruo boluomiduo xin jing (般若波羅蜜多心經)	251
Skt.	Prajñāpāramitāhṛdaya-sūtra	
Ch.	Miaofa lianhua jing (妙法蓮華經)	262
Skt.	Saddharmapuṇḍarīka-sūtra	
Eng.	*The Lotus Sutra* (Revised Second Edition, 2007)	
Ch.	Wuliangyi jing (無量義經)	276
Eng.	*The Infinite Meanings Sutra* (in *Tiantai Lotus Texts,* 2013)	
Ch.	Guan Puxian pusa xingfa jing (觀普賢菩薩行法經)	277
Eng.	*The Sutra Expounded by the Buddha on Practice of the Way through Contemplation of the Bodhisattva All-embracing Goodness* (in *Tiantai Lotus Texts,* 2013)	
Ch.	Dafangguang fo huayan jing (大方廣佛華嚴經)	279
Skt.	Avataṃsaka-sūtra	
Ch.	Shengman shizihou yisheng dafang bianfang guang jing (勝鬘師子吼一乘大方便方廣經)	353
Skt.	Śrīmālādevīsiṃhanāda-sūtra	
Eng.	*The Sutra of Queen Śrīmālā of the Lion's Roar* (2004)	
Ch.	Wuliangshou jing (無量壽經)	360
Skt.	Sukhāvatīvyūha	
Eng.	*The Larger Sutra on Amitāyus* (in *The Three Pure Land Sutras,* Revised Second Edition, 2003)	
Ch.	Guan wuliangshou fo jing (觀無量壽佛經)	365
Skt.	*Amitāyurdhyāna-sūtra	
Eng.	*The Sutra on Contemplation of Amitāyus* (in *The Three Pure Land Sutras,* Revised Second Edition, 2003)	
Ch.	Amituo jing (阿彌陀經)	366
Skt.	Sukhāvatīvyūha	
Eng.	*The Smaller Sutra on Amitāyus* (in *The Three Pure Land Sutras,* Revised Second Edition, 2003)	

Title		Taishō No.
Ch.	Da banniepan jing (大般涅槃經)	374
Skt.	Mahāparinirvāṇa-sūtra	
Eng.	*The Nirvana Sutra* (Volume I, 2013)	
Ch.	Fochuibo niepan lüeshuo jiaojie jing (佛垂般涅槃略説教誡經)	389
Eng.	*The Bequeathed Teaching Sutra* (in *Apocryphal Scriptures,* 2005)	
Ch.	Dizang pusa benyuan jing (地藏菩薩本願經)	412
Skt.	*Kṣitigarbhapraṇidhāna-sūtra	
Ch.	Banzhou sanmei jing (般舟三昧經)	418
Skt.	Pratyutpanna-buddhasammukhāvasthita-samādhi-sūtra	
Eng.	*The Pratyutpanna Samādhi Sutra* (1998)	
Ch.	Yaoshi liuli guang rulai benyuan gongde jing (藥師琉璃光如來本願功德經)	450
Skt.	Bhaiṣajyaguru-vaiḍūrya-prabhāsa-pūrvapraṇidhāna-viśeṣavistara	
Ch.	Mile xiasheng chengfo jing (彌勒下生成佛經)	454
Skt.	*Maitreyavyākaraṇa	
Ch.	Wenshushili wen jing (文殊師利問經)	468
Skt.	*Mañjuśrīparipṛcchā	
Ch.	Weimojie suoshuo jing (維摩詰所説經)	475
Skt.	Vimalakīrtinirdeśa-sūtra	
Eng.	*The Vimalakīrti Sutra* (2004)	
Ch.	Yueshangnü jing (月上女經)	480
Skt.	Candrottarādārikā-paripṛcchā	
Ch.	Zuochan sanmei jing (坐禪三昧經)	614
Eng.	*The Sutra on the Concentration of Sitting Meditation* (2009)	
Ch.	Damoduoluo chan jing (達磨多羅禪經)	618
Ch.	Yuedeng sanmei jing (月燈三昧經)	639
Skt.	Samādhirāja-candrapradīpa-sūtra	
Ch.	Shoulengyan sanmei jing (首楞嚴三昧經)	642
Skt.	Śūraṅgamasamādhi-sūtra	
Eng.	*The Śūraṅgama Samādhi Sutra* (1998)	
Ch.	Jinguang ming zuishengwang jing (金光明最勝王經)	665
Skt.	Suvarṇaprabhāsa-sūtra	

Title	Taishō No.
Ch. Dasheng rulengqie jing (大乘入楞伽經)	672
Skt. Laṅkāvatāra-sūtra	
Ch. Jie shenmi jing (解深密經)	676
Skt. Saṃdhinirmocana-sūtra	
Eng. *The Scripture on the Explication of Underlying Meaning* (2000)	
Ch. Yulanpen jing (盂蘭盆經)	685
Skt. *Ullambana-sūtra	
Eng. *The Ullambana Sutra* (in *Apocryphal Scriptures,* 2005)	
Ch. Sishierzhang jing (四十二章經)	784
Eng. *The Sutra of Forty-two Sections* (in *Apocryphal Scriptures,* 2005)	
Ch. Dafangguang yuanjue xiuduoluo liaoyi jing (大方廣圓覺修多羅了義經)	842
Eng. *The Sutra of Perfect Enlightenment* (in *Apocryphal Scriptures,* 2005)	
Ch. Da Biluzhena chengfo shenbian jiachi jing (大毘盧遮那成佛神變加持經)	848
Skt. Mahāvairocanābhisambodhi-vikurvitādhiṣṭhāna-vaipulyasūtrendra-rājanāma-dharmaparyāya	
Eng. *The Vairocanābhisaṃbodhi Sutra* (2005)	
Ch. Jinggangding yiqie rulai zhenshi she dasheng xianzheng dajiao wang jing (金剛頂一切如來眞實攝大乘現證大教王經)	865
Skt. Sarvatathāgata-tattvasaṃgraha-mahāyānābhisamaya-mahākalparāja	
Eng. *The Adamantine Pinnacle Sutra* (in *Two Esoteric Sutras,* 2001)	
Ch. Suxidi jieluo jing (蘇悉地羯囉經)	893
Skt. Susiddhikara-mahātantra-sādhanopāyika-paṭala	
Eng. *The Susiddhikara Sutra* (in *Two Esoteric Sutras,* 2001)	
Ch. Modengqie jing (摩登伽經)	1300
Skt. *Mātaṅgī-sūtra	
Eng. *The Mātaṅga Sutra* (in *Esoteric Texts,* 2015)	
Ch. Mohe sengqi lü (摩訶僧祇律)	1425
Skt. *Mahāsāṃghika-vinaya	
Ch. Sifen lü (四分律)	1428
Skt. *Dharmaguptaka-vinaya	

Title		Taishō No.
Ch.	Shanjianlü piposha (善見律毘婆沙)	1462
Pāli	Samantapāsādikā	
Ch.	Fanwang jing (梵網經)	1484
Skt.	*Brahmajāla-sūtra	
Ch.	Youposaijie jing (優婆塞戒經)	1488
Skt.	Upāsakaśīla-sūtra	
Eng.	*The Sutra on Upāsaka Precepts* (1994)	
Ch.	Miaofa lianhua jing youbotishe (妙法蓮華經憂波提舍)	1519
Skt.	Saddharmapuṇḍarīka-upadeśa	
Eng.	*The Commentary on the Lotus Sutra* (in *Tiantai Lotus Texts,* 2013)	
Ch.	Shizha biposha lun (十住毘婆沙論)	1521
Skt.	*Daśabhūmika-vibhāṣā	
Ch.	Fodijing lun (佛地經論)	1530
Skt.	*Buddhabhūmisūtra-śāstra	
Eng.	*The Interpretation of the Buddha Land* (2002)	
Ch.	Apidamojushe lun (阿毘達磨俱舍論)	1558
Skt.	Abhidharmakośa-bhāṣya	
Ch.	Zhonglun (中論)	1564
Skt.	Madhyamaka-śāstra	
Ch.	Yüqie shidilun (瑜伽師地論)	1579
Skt.	Yogācārabhūmi-śāstra	
Ch.	Cheng weishi lun (成唯識論)	1585
Eng.	*Demonstration of Consciousness Only* (in *Three Texts on Consciousness Only,* 1999)	
Ch.	Weishi sanshilun song (唯識三十論頌)	1586
Skt.	Triṃśikā	
Eng.	*The Thirty Verses on Consciousness Only* (in *Three Texts on Consciousness Only,* 1999)	
Ch.	Weishi ershi lun (唯識二十論)	1590
Skt.	Viṃśatikā	
Eng.	*The Treatise in Twenty Verses on Consciousness Only* (in *Three Texts on Consciousness Only,* 1999)	

Title		Taishō No.
Ch.	She dasheng lun (攝大乘論)	1593
Skt.	Mahāyānasaṃgraha	
Eng.	*The Summary of the Great Vehicle* (Revised Second Edition, 2003)	
Ch.	Bian zhongbian lun (辯中邊論)	1600
Skt.	Madhyāntavibhāga	
Ch.	Dasheng zhuangyanjing lun (大乘莊嚴經論)	1604
Skt.	Mahāyānasūtrālaṃkāra	
Ch.	Dasheng chengye lun (大乘成業論)	1609
Skt.	Karmasiddhiprakaraṇa	
Ch.	Jiujing yisheng baoxing lun (究竟一乘寶性論)	1611
Skt.	Ratnagotravibhāga-mahāyānottaratantra-śāstra	
Ch.	Yinming ruzheng li lun (因明入正理論)	1630
Skt.	Nyāyapraveśa	
Ch.	Dasheng ji pusa xue lun (大乘集菩薩學論)	1636
Skt.	Śikṣāsamuccaya	
Ch.	Jingangzhen lun (金剛針論)	1642
Skt.	Vajrasūcī	
Ch.	Zhang suozhi lun (彰所知論)	1645
Eng.	*The Treatise on the Elucidation of the Knowable* (2004)	
Ch.	Putixing jing (菩提行經)	1662
Skt.	Bodhicaryāvatāra	
Ch.	Jingangding yuqie zhongfa anouduoluo sanmiao sanputi xin lun (金剛頂瑜伽中發阿耨多羅三藐三菩提心論)	1665
Eng.	*The Bodhicitta Śāstra* (in *Esoteric Texts,* 2015)	
Ch.	Dasheng qixin lun (大乘起信論)	1666
Skt.	*Mahāyānaśraddhotpāda-śāstra	
Eng.	*The Awakening of Faith* (2005)	
Ch.	Shimoheyan lun (釋摩訶衍論)	1668
Ch.	Naxian biqiu jing (那先比丘經)	1670
Pāli	Milindapañha	
Ch.	Banruo boluomiduo xin jing yuzan (般若波羅蜜多心經幽賛)	1710
Eng.	*A Comprehensive Commentary on the Heart Sutra (Prajñāpāramitā-hṛdaya-sūtra)* (2001)	

Title		Taishō No.
Ch.	Miaofalianhua jing xuanyi (妙法蓮華經玄義)	1716
Ch.	Guan wuliangshou fo jing shu (觀無量壽佛經疏)	1753
Ch.	Sanlun xuanyi (三論玄義)	1852
Ch.	Dasheng xuan lun (大乘玄論)	1853
Ch.	Zhao lun (肇論)	1858
Ch.	Huayan yisheng jiaoyi fenqi zhang (華嚴一乘教義分齊章)	1866
Ch.	Yuanren lun (原人論)	1886
Ch.	Mohe zhiguan (摩訶止觀)	1911
Ch.	Xiuxi zhiguan zuochan fayao (修習止觀坐禪法要)	1915
Ch.	Tiantai sijiao yi (天台四教儀)	1931
Eng.	*A Guide to the Tiantai Fourfold Teachings* (in *Tiantai Lotus Texts,* 2013)	
Ch.	Guoqing bai lu (國清百録)	1934
Ch.	Zhenzhou Linji Huizhao chanshi wulu (鎭州臨濟慧照禪師語録)	1985
Eng.	*The Recorded Sayings of Linji* (in *Three Chan Classics,* 1999)	
Ch.	Foguo Yuanwu chanshi biyan lu (佛果圜悟禪師碧巖録)	2003
Eng.	*The Blue Cliff Record* (1998)	
Ch.	Wumen guan (無門關)	2005
Eng.	*Wumen's Gate* (in *Three Chan Classics,* 1999)	
Ch.	Liuzu dashi fabao tan jing (六祖大師法寶壇經)	2008
Eng.	*The Platform Sutra of the Sixth Patriarch* (2000)	
Ch.	Xinxin ming (信心銘)	2010
Eng.	*The Faith-Mind Maxim* (in *Three Chan Classics,* 1999)	
Ch.	Huangboshan Duanji chanshi chuanxin fayao (黃檗山斷際禪師傳心法要)	2012A
Eng.	*Essentials of the Transmission of Mind* (in *Zen Texts,* 2005)	
Ch.	Yongjia Zhengdao ge (永嘉證道歌)	2014
Ch.	Chixiu Baizhang qinggui (勅修百丈清規)	2025
Eng.	*The Baizhang Zen Monastic Regulations* (2007)	

Title	Taishō No.
Ch. Yibuzonglun lun (異部宗輪論) Skt. Samayabhedoparacanacakra Eng. *The Cycle of the Formation of the Schismatic Doctrines* (2004)	2031
Ch. Ayuwang jing (阿育王經) Skt. Aśokāvadāna Eng. *The Biographical Scripture of King Aśoka* (1993)	2043
Ch. Maming pusa zhuan (馬鳴菩薩傳) Eng. *The Life of Aśvaghoṣa Bodhisattva* (in *Lives of Great Monks and Nuns,* 2002)	2046
Ch. Longshu pusa zhuan (龍樹菩薩傳) Eng. *The Life of Nāgārjuna Bodhisattva* (in *Lives of Great Monks and Nuns,* 2002)	2047
Ch. Posoupandou fashi zhuan (婆藪槃豆法師傳) Eng. *Biography of Dharma Master Vasubandhu* (in *Lives of Great Monks and Nuns,* 2002)	2049
Ch. Datang Daciensi Zanzang fashi zhuan (大唐大慈恩寺三藏法師傳) Eng. *A Biography of the Tripiṭaka Master of the Great Ci'en Monastery of the Great Tang Dynasty* (1995)	2053
Ch. Gaoseng zhuan (高僧傳)	2059
Ch. Biqiuni zhuan (比丘尼傳) Eng. *Biographies of Buddhist Nuns* (in *Lives of Great Monks and Nuns,* 2002)	2063
Ch. Gaoseng Faxian zhuan (高僧法顯傳) Eng. *The Journey of the Eminent Monk Faxian* (in *Lives of Great Monks and Nuns,* 2002)	2085
Ch. Datang xiyu ji (大唐西域記) Eng. *The Great Tang Dynasty Record of the Western Regions* (1996)	2087
Ch. Youfangjichao: Tangdaheshangdongzheng zhuan (遊方記抄: 唐大和上東征傳)	2089-(7)
Ch. Hongming ji (弘明集) Eng. *The Collection for the Propagation and Clarification of Buddhism* (Volume I, 2015)	2102
Ch. Fayuan zhulin (法苑珠林)	2122

Title		Taishō No.
Ch.	Nanhai jigui neifa zhuan (南海寄歸内法傳)	2125
Eng.	*Buddhist Monastic Traditions of Southern Asia* (2000)	
Ch.	Fanyu zaming (梵語雑名)	2135
Jp.	Shōmangyō gisho (勝鬘經義疏)	2185
Eng.	*Prince Shōtoku's Commentary on the Śrīmālā Sutra* (2011)	
Jp.	Yuimakyō gisho (維摩經義疏)	2186
Eng.	*The Expository Commentary on the Vimalakīrti Sutra* (2012)	
Jp.	Hokke gisho (法華義疏)	2187
Jp.	Hannya shingyō hiken (般若心經秘鍵)	2203
Jp.	Daijō hossō kenjin shō (大乘法相研神章)	2309
Jp.	Kanjin kakumu shō (觀心覺夢鈔)	2312
Jp.	Risshū kōyō (律宗綱要)	2348
Eng.	*The Essentials of the Vinaya Tradition* (1995)	
Jp.	Tendai hokke shūgi shū (天台法華宗義集)	2366
Eng.	*The Collected Teachings of the Tendai Lotus School* (1995)	
Jp.	Kenkairon (顯戒論)	2376
Jp.	Sange gakushō shiki (山家學生式)	2377
Jp.	Hizōhōyaku (秘藏寶鑰)	2426
Eng.	*The Precious Key to the Secret Treasury* (in *Shingon Texts*, 2004)	
Jp.	Benkenmitsu nikyō ron (辨顯密二教論)	2427
Eng.	*On the Differences between the Exoteric and Esoteric Teachings* (in *Shingon Texts*, 2004)	
Jp.	Sokushin jōbutsu gi (即身成佛義)	2428
Eng.	*The Meaning of Becoming a Buddha in This Very Body* (in *Shingon Texts*, 2004)	
Jp.	Shōji jissōgi (聲字實相義)	2429
Eng.	*The Meanings of Sound, Sign, and Reality* (in *Shingon Texts*, 2004)	
Jp.	Unjigi (吽字義)	2430
Eng.	*The Meanings of the Word Hūṃ* (in *Shingon Texts*, 2004)	
Jp.	Gorin kuji myōhimitsu shaku (五輪九字明秘密釋)	2514
Eng.	*The Illuminating Secret Commentary on the Five Cakras and the Nine Syllables* (in *Shingon Texts*, 2004)	

Title		Taishō No.
Jp.	Mitsugonin hotsuro sange mon (密嚴院發露懺悔文)	2527
Eng.	*The Mitsugonin Confession* (in *Shingon Texts,* 2004)	
Jp.	Kōzen gokoku ron (興禪護國論)	2543
Eng.	*A Treatise on Letting Zen Flourish to Protect the State* (in *Zen Texts,* 2005)	
Jp.	Fukan zazengi (普勧坐禪儀)	2580
Eng.	*A Universal Recommendation for True Zazen* (in *Zen Texts,* 2005)	
Jp.	Shōbōgenzō (正法眼藏)	2582
Eng.	*Shōbōgenzō: The True Dharma-eye Treasury* (Volume I, 2007) *Shōbōgenzō: The True Dharma-eye Treasury* (Volume II, 2008) *Shōbōgenzō: The True Dharma-eye Treasury* (Volume III, 2008) *Shōbōgenzō: The True Dharma-eye Treasury* (Volume IV, 2008)	
Jp.	Zazen yōjin ki (坐禪用心記)	2586
Eng.	*Advice on the Practice of Zazen* (in *Zen Texts,* 2005)	
Jp.	Senchaku hongan nembutsu shū (選擇本願念佛集)	2608
Eng.	*Senchaku Hongan Nembutsu Shū: A Collection of Passages on the Nembutsu Chosen in the Original Vow* (1997)	
Jp.	Kenjōdo shinjitsu kyōgyō shōmon rui (顯淨土眞實教行証文類)	2646
Eng.	*Kyōgyōshinshō: On Teaching, Practice, Faith, and Enlightenment* (2003)	
Jp.	Tannishō (歎異抄)	2661
Eng.	*Tannishō: Passages Deploring Deviations of Faith* (1996)	
Jp.	Rennyo shōnin ofumi (蓮如上人御文)	2668
Eng.	*Rennyo Shōnin Ofumi: The Letters of Rennyo* (1996)	
Jp.	Ōjōyōshū (往生要集)	2682
Jp.	Risshō ankoku ron (立正安國論)	2688
Eng.	*Risshōankokuron or The Treatise on the Establishment of the Orthodox Teaching and the Peace of the Nation* (in *Two Nichiren Texts,* 2003)	
Jp.	Kaimokushō (開目抄)	2689
Eng.	*Kaimokushō or Liberation from Blindness* (2000)	

Title		Taishō No.
Jp.	Kanjin honzon shō (觀心本尊抄)	2692
Eng.	*Kanjinhonzonshō or The Most Venerable One Revealed by Introspecting Our Minds for the First Time at the Beginning of the Fifth of the Five Five Hundred-year Ages* (in *Two Nichiren Texts,* 2003)	
Ch.	Fumu enzhong jing (父母恩重經)	2887
Eng.	*The Sutra on the Profundity of Filial Love* (in *Apocryphal Scriptures,* 2005)	
Jp.	Hasshūkōyō (八宗綱要)	extracanonical
Eng.	*The Essentials of the Eight Traditions* (1994)	
Jp.	Sangō shīki (三教指帰)	extracanonical
Jp.	Mappō tōmyō ki (末法燈明記)	extracanonical
Eng.	*The Candle of the Latter Dharma* (1994)	
Jp.	Jūshichijō kenpō (十七條憲法)	extracanonical

Title		Taishō No.
Jp.	Kanjin honzon shō (觀心本尊抄)	2692
Eng.	*Kanjinhonzonshō or The Most Venerable One Revealed by Introspecting Our Minds for the First Time at the Beginning of the Fifth of the Five Five Hundred-year Ages* (in *Two Nichiren Texts,* 2003)	
Ch.	Fumu enzhong jing (父母恩重經)	2887
Eng.	*The Sutra on the Profundity of Filial Love* (in *Apocryphal Scriptures,* 2005)	
Jp.	Hasshūkōyō (八宗綱要)	extracanonical
Eng.	*The Essentials of the Eight Traditions* (1994)	
Jp.	Sangō shīki (三教指帰)	extracanonical
Jp.	Mappō tōmyō ki (末法燈明記)	extracanonical
Eng.	*The Candle of the Latter Dharma* (1994)	
Jp.	Jūshichijō kenpō (十七條憲法)	extracanonical